TOM SLADE AT
TEMPLE CAMP

PERCY K. FITZHUGH

1st WORLD
LIBRARY
Literary Society

Tom Slade at Temple Camp

Percy K. Fitzhugh

© 1st World Library, 2009
PO Box 2211
Fairfield, IA 52556
www.1stworldlibrary.com
First Edition

LCCN: 2009923485

Softcover ISBN: 978-1-4218-8871-2
Hardcover ISBN: 978-1-4218-8970-2
eBook ISBN: 978-1-4218-8772-2

Purchase *"Tom Slade at Temple Camp"*
as a traditional bound book at:
www.1stWorldLibrary.com/purchase.asp?ISBN=978-1-4218-8871-2

1st World Library is a literary, educational organization
dedicated to:

- Creating a free internet library of downloadable ebooks

- Hosting writing competitions and offering book publishing
scholarships.

Interested in more 1st World Library books? contact:
literacy@1stworldlibrary.com

Check us out at: www.1stworldlibrary.com

1st World Library Literary Society

Giving Back to the World

"If you want to work on the core problem, it's early school literacy."

- James Barksdale, former CEO of Netscape

"No skill is more crucial to the future of a child, or to a democratic and prosperous society, than literacy."

- Los Angeles Times

"Literacy... means far more than learning how to read and write... The aim is to transmit... knowledge and promote social participation."

- UNESCO

"Literacy is not a luxury, it is a right and a responsibility. If our world is to meet the challenges of the twenty-first century we must harness the energy and creativity of all our citizens."

- President Bill Clinton

"Parents should be encouraged to read to their children, and teachers should be equipped with all available techniques for teaching literacy, so the varying needs and capacities of individual kids can be taken into account."

- Hugh Mackay

TABLE OF CONTENTS

CHAPTER I

ROY'S SACRIFICE

"Rejected by a large majority—I mean, elected by a large majority."

Roy Blakeley gathered up the ballots in his two hands, dropped them into the shoe box and pushed the box across the table to Mr. Ellsworth as if the matter were finally settled.

"Honorable Roy Blakeley," he added, "didn't even carry his own patrol."

This humiliating confession, offered in Roy's gayest manner, was true. The Silver Foxes had turned from their leader and, to a scout, voted for Tom Slade. It was hinted that Roy himself was responsible for this, but he was a good politician and would not talk. There was also a dark rumor that a certain young lady was mixed up in the matter and it is a fact that only the night before Roy and Mary Temple had been seen in earnest converse on the wide veranda at Grantley Square by Pee-wee Harris, who believed that a scout should be observant.

Be this as it may, Tom had carried his own patrol, the Elks, unanimously, and the Silver Foxes had voted for him like instructed delegates, while among the proud and dignified Ravens there had been but one dissenting vote. Someone had cast this for Pee-wee Harris, the Silver Fox mascot and the troop's chief exhibit. But, of course, it was only a joke. The idea of Pee-wee going away as assistant camp manager was preposterous. Why, you could hardly see him without a magnifying glass.

"If this particular majority had been much larger," announced Roy, "it wouldn't have been a majority at all; it would have been a unanimity."

"A una *what*?" someone asked.

"A unanimity—that's Latin for home run. Seems a pity that the only thing that prevented a clean sweep was a little three-foot pocket edition of a boy scout—"

At this moment, Pee-wee, by a miracle of dexterity, landed a ball of twine plunk in the middle of Roy's face.

"Roy," laughed Mr. Ellsworth, "you're a good campaign manager."

"He's a boss," shouted Pee-wee, "that's what he is. A boss is a feller that has people elected and then makes them do what he says."

"Well, you were glad enough to vote for him with the rest, weren't you?" laughed the scoutmaster.

And Pee-wee had to confess that he was.

But there was no doubt that Roy had managed the whole thing, and if ever political boss saw his fondest wishes realized Roy did now.

"I think," said Mr. Ellsworth, "that it is up to Tom to deliver his speech of acceptance."

"Sure it is," said Westy Martin (Silver Fox). "We want to know his policies. Is he going to favor the Elks or is he going to be neutral?"

"Is he for troop first or camp first?" asked Doc. Carson (Raven and First-aid scout).

"Is Roy Blakeley going to come in for three or four helpings at mess because he ran the campaign?" asked Connie Bennett, of the new Elks.

"Speech, speech!" called Eddie Ingram, of the Silver Foxes.

Tom looked uneasily at Mr. Ellsworth and on the scout-master's laughing nod of encouragement arose.

He was not at his best in a thing of this kind; he had always envied Roy his easy, bantering manner, but he was not the one to shirk a duty, so he stood up.

He was about fifteen and of a heavy, ungraceful build. His hair was thick and rather scraggly, his face was of the square type, and his expression what people call stolid. He had freckles but not too many, and his mouth was large and his lips tight-set. His face wore a characteristic frown which was the last feeble trace of a lowering look which had once disfigured it. Frowns are in the taboo list of the scouts, but somehow this one wasn't half bad; there was a kind of rugged strength in it. He wore khaki trousers and a brown flannel shirt which was unbuttoned in front, exposing an expanse of very brown chest.

For Tom Slade's virtues you will have to plow through these pages if you have not already met him, but for his faults, they were printed all over him like cities on a map. He was stubborn, rather reticent, sometimes unreasonable, and carried with him that air of stolid self-confidence which is apt to be found in one who has surmounted obstacles and risen in spite of handicaps. It was often said in the troop that one never knew how to take Tom.

"I think Pee-wee is right," he said, "and I guess Roy managed this. I could see he was doing some private wig-wag work, and I think you've all been—what d'you call it—co-something or other—"

"Coerced!" suggested Pee-wee.

(Cries of "No, you're crazy!")

"But as long as I'm elected I'll take the job—and I'm very thankful. I won't deny I wanted it. Roy won't get any favors." (Cheers) "If I have any deciding to do I'll decide the way I think is right. That's all I've got to say—oh, yes, there's one thing more—one thing I made up my mind to in case I was lucky enough to get elected." (Cries of "Hear, hear!") "I'm not going to go by the railroad. I got an idea, like, that it doesn't took right for a scout to go to camp by train. So I'm going to hike it up to the camp. I'm going to start early enough so I can do it. When a scout steps off a train he looks like a summer boarder. I ask Roy to go with me if he can start when I do. I don't want you fellows to think I was expecting to be chosen. I didn't let myself think about it. But sometimes you can't help thinking about a thing; and the other night I said to myself that if anything should happen I should get elected—"

(A voice, "You didn't do a thing but walk away with

Percy K. Fitzhugh

it, Tommy!")

(Cries of "Shut up till he gets through!")

"I wouldn't go to that camp in a train. I'm not going to set foot in it till I'm qualified for a first-class scout, and I'm going to do the rest of my stunts on the way. I want Roy to go with me if he can. I thank you for electing me. I'll do my best in that job. If I knew how to say it, I'd thank you better. I guess I'm kind of rattled."

The blunt little speech was very characteristic of Tom and it was greeted with a storm of applause. He had a way of blurting out his plans and ideas without giving any previous hint of them, but this was something of a knockout blow.

"Oh, you hit it right!" shouted Pee-wee. "Gee, I do hate railroad trains—railroad trains and homework."

"You don't mean you're going to hike it from here, Tom, do you?" asked Mr. Ellsworth.

"I had an idea I might canoe up as far as Nyack," said Tom, "and then follow the river up to Catskill Landing and hit in for Leeds—but, of course," he added, "I didn't really expect to be elected."

"Oh, crinkums!" shouted Pee-wee. "I'll go with you!"

"Well," said Roy, when the laughter had subsided, "this is a new wrinkle and it sounds rather risky for a half-baked Elk—" (Hisses from the Elks) "So far as I'm concerned, I think a hike of a hundred miles or so—"

"You're crazy!" interrupted Pee-wee. "You silver-plated Fox—"

"Is too much," concluded Roy. "In the first place, there would have to be a whole lot of discomfort." (Hisses) "A fellow would be pretty sure to get his feet wet." (Mr. Ellsworth restrained Pee-wee with difficulty.) "He would have to sleep out of doors in the damp night air—" (A voice, "Slap him on the wrist!") "And he would be likely to get lost. Scouts, it's no fun to be lost in the woods—" (Cries of "Yes, it is!") "We would be footsore and weary," continued Roy.

"You got that out of a book!" shouted Pee-wee. "*Footsore and weary*—that's the way folks talk in books!"

"We might be caught in the rain," said Roy, soberly. "We might have to pick our way along obscure trail or up steep mountains."

"You ought to go and take a ride in a merry-go-round," cried Pee-wee, sarcastically.

"In short, it is fraught with peril," said Roy.

"You got *that* out of a book, too," said Pee-wee, disgustedly, "*fraught with peril*!"

"I think it is too much of an undertaking," said Roy, ignoring him. "We can get round-trip tickets."

Pee-wee almost fell off his chair.

"But, of course," continued Roy, soberly, "a scout is not supposed to think of himself—especially a Silver Fox. I am a Silver Fox—sterling—warranted. A scout is a brother to every other scout. He ought to be ready to make sacrifices." (Mr. Ellsworth began to chuckle.)

"He ought not to stand by and see a fellow scout in danger. He ought not to stand and see a poor Elk go headlong—" (Hisses) "He ought to be ready with a good turn regardless of his own comfort and safety." (Hoots and laughter) "I am ready with a good turn. I am ready to sac—" (Jeers) "I am ready to sac—" (Jeers) "I am—" (Cries of "Noble lad!") "I am ready to sac—"

"Well, go ahead and *sac*, why don't you?" shouted Pee-wee in disgust. "You're a hyp—"

"Hip—hooray!" concluded several scouts.

"You're a hyp—hyp—hypocrite!" Pee-wee managed to ejaculate amid the tumult.

"I am ready to sac—"

"Oh, go on, sac and be done with it!"

"I am ready to sacrifice myself for Tom Slade," finished Roy, magnanimously. "Tom," he added, extending his hand across the table with a noble air of martyrdom, "Tom, I will go with you!"

The meeting broke up gaily, Mr. Ellsworth saying that he would certainly communicate Roy's generous and self-sacrificing offer to National Headquarters as a conspicuous instance of a memorable and epoch-making good turn.

"He gets my goat!" said Pee-wee to the scoutmaster.

"I am very glad," said Mr. Ellsworth, soberly, "that our summer begins with a good turn. The Silver Foxes should be proud of their unselfish leader." Then he turned to Doc.

Carson and winked the other eye.

He was a great jollier—Mr. Ellsworth.

Percy K. Fitzhugh

CHAPTER II

INDIAN SCOUT SIGN

[Transcriber's Note: An Indian scout sign drawing was inserted here.]

The old Indian scout sign, which is the title of this chapter, means *There is nothing new along this trail and it brings you back to the same place.* If you are already acquainted with Tom Slade and his friends you will be safe in skipping this chapter but, otherwise, you would better read it for it will tell you a little of Tom's past history and of the other scouts with whom you are to become acquainted in this volume.

To know just how all this election business came about we must go back a year or so to a time when Tom Slade was just a hoodlum down in Barrel Alley and believed with all his heart that the best use a barrel stave could be put to was to throw it into the Chinese laundry. He had heard of the Boy Scouts and he called them "regiment guys" and had a sophisticated contempt for them.

Then all of a sudden, along had come Roy Blakeley, who had shown him that he was just wasting good barrel staves; that you could make a first-class Indian bow out of a barrel stave. Roy had also told him that you can't smoke cigarettes if you expect to aim straight. That was an end of the barrel as a missile and that was an end of *Turkish Blend Mixture*—or whatever you call it. There wasn't any talk or preaching—just a couple of good knockout blows.

Tom had held that of all the joys in the mischievous hoodlum program none was so complete as that of throwing chunks of coal through streetcar windows at the passengers inside. Then along had come Westy Martin and shown him how you could mark patrol signs on rocks with chunks of coal—signs which should guide the watchful scout through the trackless wilderness. Exit coal as a missile.

In short, Tom Slade awoke to the realization not only that he was a hoodlum, but that he was out of date with his vulgar slang and bungling, unskilful tricks.

Tom and his father had lived in two rooms in one of John Temple's tenements down in Barrel Alley and John Temple and his wife and daughter lived in a couple of dozen rooms, a few lawns, porches, sun-parlors and things up in Grantley Square. And John Temple stood a better chance of being struck by lightning than of collecting the rent from Bill Slade.

John Temple was very rich and very grouchy. He owned the Bridgeboro National Bank; he owned all the vacant lots with their hospitable "Keep Out" signs, and he had a controlling interest in pretty nearly everything else in town—except his own temper.

Poor, lazy Bill Slade and his misguided son might have gone on living in John Temple's tenement rent free until it fell in a heap, for though Mr. Temple blustered he was not bad at heart; but on an evil day Tom had thrown a rock at Bridgeboro's distinguished citizen. It was a random, unscientific shot but, as luck would have it, it knocked John Temple's new golf cap off into the rich mud of Barrel Alley.

It did not hurt John Temple, but it killed the goose that laid the golden eggs for the Slades. Mr. Temple's dignity was more than hurt; it was black and blue. He would rather have been hit by a financial panic than by that sordid missile from Barrel Alley's most notorious hoodlum. Inside of three days out went the Slades from John Temple's tenement, bag and baggage.

There wasn't much baggage. A couple of broken chairs, a greasy dining-table which Tom had used strategically in his defensive operations against his father's assaults, a dented beer-can and a few other dilapidated odds and ends constituted the household effects of the unfortunate father and son.

Bill Slade, unable to cope with this unexpected disaster, disappeared on the day of the eviction and Tom was sheltered by a kindly neighbor, Mrs. O'Connor.

His fortunes were at the very lowest ebb and it seemed a fairly safe prophesy that he would presently land in the Home for Wayward Boys, when one day he met Roy Blakeley and tried to hold him up for a nickel.

Far be it from me to defend the act, but it was about the best thing that Tom ever did so far as his own interests were concerned. Roy took him up to his own little Camp Solitaire on the beautiful lawn of the Blakeley home, gave him a cup of coffee, some plum duff (Silver Fox brand, patent applied for), and passed him out some of the funniest slang (all brand new) that poor Tom had ever heard.

That was the beginning of Tom's transformation into a scout. He fell for scouting with a vengeance. It opened up a new world to him. To be sure, this king of the hoodlums did not capitulate all at once—not he. He was still wary of all "rich guys" and "sissies"; but he used to go down and peek through a hole in the fence of Temple's lot when they were practising their games.

Mr. Ellsworth said nothing, only winked his eye at the boys, for he saw which way the wind was blowing. Tom Slade, king of the hoodlums, had the scout bug and didn't know it.

Then, when the time was ripe, Mr. Ellsworth called him down into the field one day for a try at archery. Tom scrambled down from the fence and shuffled over to where the scouts waited with smiling, friendly faces; but just at that moment, who should come striding through the field but John Temple—straight for the little group.

What happened was not pleasant. John Temple denounced them all as a gang of trespassers, ordered them out of his field and did not hesitate to express his opinion of Tom in particular. Mr. Ellsworth then and there championed the poor fellow and prophesied that notwithstanding his past the scouts would make a man of him yet.

After that Tom Slade came out flat-footed and hit the scout trail. He was never able to determine to whom he should be most grateful, Roy Blakeley or Mr. Ellsworth, but it was the beginning of a friendship between the two boys which became closer as time passed.

There is no use retelling a tale that is told. Tom had such a summer in camp as he had never dreamed of when he used to lie in bed till noontime in Barrel Alley, and all that you shall find in its proper place, but you must know something of how Temple Camp came into being and how it came by its name.

Percy K. Fitzhugh

John Temple was a wonderful man—oh, he was smart. He could take care of your property for you; if you had a thousand dollars he would turn it into two thousand for you—like a sleight-of-hand performer. He could tell you what kind of stocks to buy and when to sell them. He knew where to buy real estate. He could tell you when wheat was going up or down—just as if there were a scout sign to go by. He had everything that heart could wish—and the rheumatism besides.

But his dubious prophesy as to the future of Tom Slade, king of the hoodlums, came out all wrong. Tom was instrumental in getting back a pin which had been stolen from Mary Temple, and when her father saw the boy after six months or so of scouting he couldn't have been more surprised—not even if the Bridgeboro Bank had failed.

Then poor old John Temple (or rich old John Temple) showed that he had one good scout trait. He could be a good loser. He saw that he was all wrong and that Mr. Ellsworth was right and he straightway built a pavilion for the scouts in the beautiful woods where all the surprising episodes of the summer which had opened his eyes had taken place.

But you know as well as I do that a man like John Temple would never be satisfied with building a little one-troop camping pavilion; not he. So what should he do but buy a tract of land up in the Catskills close to a beautiful sheet of water which was called Black Lake; and here he put up a big open shack with a dozen or so log cabins about it and endowed the whole thing as a summer camp where troops from all over the country might come and find accommodations and recreation in the summer months.

That was not all. Temple Camp was to be a school where scouting might be taught (Oh, he was going to do the right thing, was old John Temple!), and to that end he communicated with somebody who communicated with somebody else, who got in touch with somebody else who went to some ranch or other a hundred miles from nowhere in the woolly west and asked old Jeb Rushmore if he wouldn't come east and look after this big scout camp. How in the world John Temple, in his big leather chair in the Bridgeboro Bank, had ever got wind of Jeb Rushmore no one was able to find out. John Temple was a genius for picking out men and in this case he touched high-water mark.

Jeb Rushmore was furnished with passes over all John Temple's railroads straight through from somewhere or other in Dakota to Catskill Landing, and a funny sight he must have been in his flannel shirt and slouch hat, sprawling his lanky limbs from the platforms of observation cars, drawling out his pithy observations about the civilization which he had never before seen.

There are only two more things necessary to mention in this "side trail" chapter. Tom's father bobbed up after the boy had become a scout. He was a mere shadow of his former self; drink and a wandering life had all but completed his ruin, and although Tom and his companions gave him a home in their pleasant camp it was too late to help him much and he died among them, having seen (if it were any satisfaction for him to see) that scouting had made a splendid boy of his once neglected son.

This brings us to the main trail again and explains why it was that Roy Blakeley had held mysterious conferences with Mary Temple, and suggested to all the three patrols that it would be a good idea to elect Tom to go to Temple Camp to assist in its preparation and management. They had all known that one of their number was to be chosen for this post and Roy had hit on Tom as the one to go because he still lived with Mrs. O'Connor down in Barrel Alley and had not the same pleasant home surroundings as the other boys.

A scout is thoughtful.

CHAPTER III

PEE-WEE AND MARY TEMPLE

Throughout the previous summer Tom had been in Roy's patrol, the Silver Foxes, but when the new Elk Patrol was formed with Connie Bennett, the Bronson boys and others, he had been chosen its leader.

"I think it's just glorious," said Mary Temple, when Tom told her of his plan and of Roy's noble sacrifice, "and I wish I was a boy."

"Oh, it's great to be a boy," enthused Pee-wee. "Gee, that's one thing I'm glad of anyway—that I'm a boy!"

"Half a boy is better than all girl," taunted Roy.

"*You're* a model boy," added Westy.

"And mother and father and I are coming up in the touring car in August to visit the camp," said Mary. "Oh, I think it's perfectly lovely you and Tom are going on ahead and that you're going to walk, and you'll have everything ready when the others get there. Good-bye."

Tom and Roy were on their way up to the Blakeley place to

set about preparing for the hike, for they meant to start as soon as they could get ready. Pee-wee lingered upon the veranda at Temple Court swinging his legs from the rubble-stone coping—those same legs that had made the scout pace famous.

"Oh, crinkums," he said, "they'll have *some* time! Cracky, but I'd like to go. You don't believe all this about Roy's making a *noble sacrifice*, do you?" he added, scornfully.

Mary laughed and said she didn't.

"Because that isn't a good turn," Pee-wee argued, anxious that Mary should not get a mistaken notion of this important phase of scouting. "A good turn is when you do something that helps somebody else. If you do it because you get a lot of fun out of it yourself, then it isn't a good turn at all. Of course, Roy knows that; he's only jollying when he calls it a good turn. You have to be careful with Roy, he's a terrible jollier—and Mr. Ellsworth's pretty near as bad. Oh, cracky, but I'd like to go with them—that's one sure thing. You think it's no fun being a girl and I'll admit *I* wouldn't want to be one—I got to admit that; but it's pretty near as bad to be small. If you're small they jolly you. And if I asked them to let me go they'd only laugh. Gee, I don't mind being jollied, but I *would* like to go. That's one thing you ought to be thankful for—you're not small. Of course, maybe girls can't do so many things as boys—I mean scouting-like—but—oh, crinkums," he broke off in an ecstasy of joyous reflection. "Oh, crinkums, that'll be some trip, *believe me.*"

Mary Temple looked at the diminutive figure in khaki trousers which sat before her on the coping. It was one of the good things about Pee-wee Harris that he never dreamed how much people liked him.

"I don't know about that," said Mary. "I mean about a girl not being able to do things—scouting things. Mightn't a girl do a good turn?"

"Oh, sure," Pee-wee conceded.

"But I suppose if it gave her very much pleasure it wouldn't be a good turn."

"Oh, yes, it might," admitted Pee-wee, anxious to explain the science of good turns. "This is the way it is. If you do a good turn it's sure to make you feel good—that you did it—see? But if you do it just for your own pleasure, then it's not a good turn. But Roy puts over a lot of nonsense about good turns. He does it just to make me mad—because I've made a sort of study of them—like."

Mary laughed in spite of herself.

"He says it was a good thing when Tom threw a barrel stave in the Chinese laundry because it led to his being a scout. But that isn't logic. Do you know what logic is?"

Mary thought she had a notion of what it was.

"A thing that's bad can't be good, can it?" Pee-wee persisted. "Suppose you should hit me with a brick—"

"I wouldn't think of doing such a thing!"

"But suppose you did. And suppose the scouts came along and gave me first aid and after that I became a scout. Could you say you did me a good turn by hitting me with a brick because that way I got to be a scout? Roy—you got to be careful with him—you can't always tell when he's jollying."

Mary looked at him intently for a few seconds. "Well, then," said she, "since you've made a study of good turns tell me this. If Roy and Tom were to ask you to go with them on their long hike, would that be a good turn?"

"Sure it would, because it would have a sacrifice in it, don't you see?"

"How?"

"Because they'd do it just to please me—they wouldn't really want me."

"Well," she laughed, "Roy's good at making sacrifices."

"Je-ru-salem!" said Pee-wee, shaking his head almost incredulously at the idea of such good fortune; "that'll be some trip. But you know what they say, and it's true—I got to admit it's true—that two's a company, three's a crowd."

"It wouldn't be three," laughed Mary; "it would only be two and a half."

She watched the sturdy figure as Pee-wee trudged along the gravel walk and down the street. He seemed even smaller than he had seemed on the veranda. And it was borne in upon her how much jollying he stood for and how many good things he missed just because he *was* little, and how cheerful and generous-hearted he was withal.

The next morning Roy received a letter which read:

"Dear Roy—I want you and Tom to ask Walter Harris to go with you. Please don't tell him that I asked you. You said you were going to name one of the cabins or one of the boats for me because I took so much interest. I'd rather have you do this. You can call it a good turn if you want to—a real one.

"MARY TEMPLE."

Pee-wee Harris also received an envelope with an enclosure similar to many which he had received of late. He suspected their source. This one read as follows:

If you want to be a scout,
You must watch what you're about,
And never let a chance for mischief pass.
You may win the golden cross
If your ball you gayly toss
Through the middle of a neighbor's pane of glass.

Percy K. Fitzhugh

CHAPTER IV

TOM AND ROY

The letter from Mary Temple fell on Camp Solitaire like a thunderbolt. Camp Solitaire was the name which Roy had given his own cosy little tent on the Blakeley lawn, and here he and Tom were packing duffel bags and sharpening belt axes ready for their long tramp when the note from Grantley Square was scaled to them by the postman as he made a short cut across the lawn.

"What do you know about that?" said Roy, clearly annoyed. "We can't take *him*; he's too small. Who's going to take the responsibility? This is a team hike."

"You don't suppose he put the idea in her head, do you?" Tom asked.

"Oh, I don't know. You saw yourself how crazy he was about it."

"Pee-wee's all right," said Tom.

"Sure he's all right. He's the best little camp mascot that ever happened. But how are we going to take him along on this hike? And what's he going to do when he gets there?"

"He could help us on the troop cabin—getting it ready," Tom suggested.

Roy threw the letter aside in disgust. "That's a girl all over," he said, as he sulkily packed his duffel bag. "She doesn't think of what it means—she just wants it done, that's all, so she sends her what-d'you-call-it—edict. Pee-wee can't stand for a hundred and forty mile hike. We'd have to get a baby carriage!"

He went on with his packing, thrusting things into the depths of his duffel bag half-heartedly and with but a fraction of his usual skill. "You know as well as I do about team hikes. How can we fix this up for three *now*? We've got everything ready and made all our plans; now it seems we've got to cart this kid along or be in Dutch up at Temple's. *He* can't hike twenty miles a day. He's just got a bee in his dome that he'd like—"

"It *would* be a good turn," interrupted Tom. "I was counting on a team hike myself. I wanted to be off on a trip alone with you a while. I'm disappointed too, but it *would* be a good turn—it would be a peach of a one, so far as that's concerned."

"No, it wouldn't," contradicted Roy. "It would be a piece of blamed foolishness."

"He'd furnish some fun—he always does."

"He'd furnish a lot of trouble and responsibility! Why can't he wait and come up with the rest? Makes me sick!" Roy added, as he hurled the aluminum coffee-pot out of a chair and sat down disgustedly.

"*Now*, you see, you dented that," said Tom.

"A lot *I* care. Gee, I'd like to call the whole thing off—that's what I'd like to do. I'd do it for two cents."

"Well, I've got two cents," said Tom, "but I'm not going to offer it. *I* say, let's make the best of it. I've seen you holding your sides laughing at Pee-wee. You said yourself he was a five-reel photoplay all by himself."

Roy drew a long breath and said nothing. He was plainly in his very worst humor. He did not want Pee-wee to go. He, too, wanted to be alone with Tom. There were plenty of good turns to be done without bothering with this particular one. Besides, it was not a good turn, he told himself. It would expose Walter Harris to perils—Oh, Roy was very generous and considerate of Walter Harris—

"If it's a question of good turns," he said, "it would be a better turn to leave him home, where he'll be safe and happy. It's no good turn to him, dragging him up and down mountains till he's so dog-tired he falls all over himself—is it?"

Tom smiled a little, but said nothing.

"Oh, well, if that's the way you feel," said Roy, pulling the cord of his duffel bag so tight that it snapped, "you and Pee-wee had better go and I'll back out."

"It ain't the way I feel," said Tom, in his slow way. "I'd rather go alone with you. Didn't I say so? I guess Pee-wee thinks he's stronger than he is. *I* think he'd better be at home too and I'd rather he'd stay home, though it's mostly just because I want to be alone with you. Maybe it's selfish, but if it is I can't help it. I think sometimes a feller might do something selfish and make up for it some other way—maybe. But I don't think any feller's got a right to do something selfish and then call it a good turn. I don't believe a long hike would hurt

Pee-wee. He's the best scout-pacer in your patrol. But I want to go alone with you and I'd just as soon tell Mary so. I suppose it would be selfish, but we'd just try to make up—"

"Oh, shut up, will you!" snapped Roy. "You get on my nerves, dragging along with your theories and things. *I* don't care who goes or if anybody goes. And you can go home and sleep for all I care."

"All right," said Tom, rising. "I'd rather do that than stay here and fight. I don't see any use talking about whether it's a good turn to Pee-wee." (Roy ostentatiously busied himself with his packing and pretended not to hear.) "I wasn't thinking about Pee-wee so much anyway. It's Mary Temple that I was thinking of. It would be a good turn to her, you can't deny that. Pee-wee Harris has got nothing to do with it—it's between you and me and Mary Temple."

"You going home?" Roy asked, coldly.

"Yes."

"Well, you and Pee-wee and Mary Temple can fix it up. I'm out of it."

He took a pad and began to write, while Tom lingered in the doorway of the tent, stolid, as he always was.

"Wait and mail this for me, will you," said Roy. He wrote:

"Dear Mary—Since you butted in Tom and I have decided that it would be best for Pee-wee to go with *him* and I'll stay here. Anyway, that's what *I've* decided. So you'll get your wish, all right, and I should worry.

"ROY."

Tom took the sealed envelope, but paused irresolutely in the doorway. It was the first time that he and Roy had ever quarrelled.

"What did you say to her?" he asked.

"Never mind what I said," Roy snapped. "You'll get your wish."

"I'd rather go alone with you," said Tom, simply. "I told you that already. I'd rather see Pee-wee stay home. I care more for you," he said, hesitating a little, "than for anyone else. But I vote to take Pee-wee because Mary wants—asks—us to. I wouldn't call it a good turn leaving him home, and you wouldn't either—only you're disappointed, same as I am. I wouldn't even call it much of a good turn taking him. We can never pay back Mary Temple. It would be like giving her a cent when we owed her a thousand. I got to do what I think is right—you—you made me a scout. I—I got to be thankful to you if I can see straight. It's—it's kind of—like a—like a trail—like," he blundered on. "There can be trails in your mind, kind of. Once I chucked stones at Pee-wee and swiped Mary's ball. Now I want to take him along—a little bit for his sake, but mostly for hers. And I want to go alone with you for my own sake, because—because," he hesitated, "because I want to be alone with you. But I got to hit the right trail—you taught me that—"

"Well, go ahead and hit it," said Roy, "it's right outside the door."

Tom looked at him steadily for a few seconds as if he did not understand. You might have seen something out of the ordinary then in that stolid face. After a moment he turned and went down the hill and around the corner of the big bank building, passed Ching Woo's laundry, into which he had once thrown dirty barrel staves, picked his way through the mud of Barrel Alley and entered the door of the tenement where Mrs. O'Connor lived. He had not slept there for three nights. The sound of cats wailing and trucks rattling and babies crying was not much like the soughing of the wind in the elms up on the Blakeley lawn. But if you have hit the right trail and have a good conscience you can sleep, and Tom slept fairly well amid the din and uproar.

CHAPTER V

FIRST COUP OF THE MASCOT

Anyway, he slept better than Roy slept. All night long the leader of the Silver Foxes was haunted by that letter. The darkness, the breeze, the soothing music of crickets and locusts outside his little tent dissipated his anger, as the voices of nature are pretty sure to do, and made him see straight, to use Tom's phrase.

He thought of Tom making his lonely way back to Barrel Alley and going to bed there amid the very scenes which he had been so anxious to have him forget. He fancied him sitting on the edge of his cot in Mrs. O'Connor's stuffy dining room, reading his Scout Manual. He was always reading his Manual; he had it all marked up like a blazed trail. Roy got small consolation now from the fact that he had procured Tom's election. If Tom had been angry at him, his conscience would be easier now; but Tom seldom got mad.

In imagination he followed that letter to the Temple home. He saw it laid at Mary's place at the dining table. He saw her come dancing in to breakfast and pick it up and wave it gaily. He saw John Temple reading his paper at the head of the table and advising with Mary, who was his partner in the Temple Camp enterprise. He knew it was for her sake quite as much as for the scouts that Mr. Temple had made this splendid gift, and he knew (for he had dined at Grantley Square) just how father and daughter conferred together. Why, who was it but Mary that told John Temple there must be ten thousand wooden plates and goodness knows how many sanitary drinking cups? Mary had it all marked in the catalogues.

Roy pictured her as she opened the letter and read it,—that rude, selfish note. He wondered what she would say. And he wondered what John Temple would think. It would be such a surprise to her that poor little Pee-wee was not wanted.

In the morning Roy arose feeling very wretched after an all but sleepless night. He did not know what he should do that day. He might go up to Grantley Square and apologize, but you cannot, by apology, undo what is done.

While he was cooking his breakfast he thought of Pee-wee— Pee-wee who was always so gay and enthusiastic, who worshipped Roy, and who "did not mind being jollied." He would be ashamed to face Pee-wee even if that redoubtable scout pacer were sublimely innocent of what had taken place.

At about noon he saw Tom coming up the lawn. He looked a little shamefaced as Tom came in and sat down without a word.

"I—I was going to go down to see you," said Roy. "I—I feel different now. I can see straight. I wish I hadn't—"

"I've got a letter for you," said Tom, disinterestedly. "I was told to deliver it."

"You—were you at Temple's?"

"There isn't any answer," said Tom, with his usual exasperating stolidness.

Roy hesitated a moment. Then, as one will take a dose of medicine quickly to have it over, he grasped the envelope, tore it open, and read:

"Dear Mary—Since you butted in Tom and I have decided it would be best for Pee-wee to go with *him* and I'll stay home. Anyway, that's what *I've* decided. So you'll get your wish, all right, and I should worry.

"ROY."

He looked up into Tom's almost expressionless countenance. "Who—told—you to deliver it—Tom?"

"I told myself. You said you'd call the whole thing off for two cents. But you ought not to expect me to pay the two cents—"

"Didn't I put a stamp on it?" said Roy, looking at the envelope.

"If you want to put a stamp on it now," said Tom, "I'll go and mail it for you—but I—I didn't feel I cared to trust you for two cents—over night."

Through glistening eyes Roy looked straight at Tom, but found no response in that dogged countenance. But he knew Tom, and knew what to expect from him. "You old grouch," he shouted, running his hand through Tom's already tousled and rebellious hair. "Why don't you laugh? So you wouldn't trust me for two cents, you old Elk skinflint, wouldn't you. Well, then, the letter doesn't get mailed, that's all, for I happen to have only one stamp left and that's going to

Pee-wee Harris. Come on, get your wits to work now, and we'll send him the invitation in the form of a verse, what d'you say?"

He gave Tom such a push that even he couldn't help laughing as he staggered against the tent-pole.

"I'm no good at writing verse," said he.

"Oh, but we'll jolly the life out of that kid when we get him away," said Roy.

It is a wise precept that where ignorance is bliss, 'tis folly to be wise. Pee-wee Harris never dreamed of the discussion that had taken place as to his going, and he accepted the invitation with a glad heart.

On the momentous morning when the trio set forth upon their journey, Mary Temple, as glad as they, stood upon the steps at Grantley Square and waved them a last good-bye.

"Don't forget," she called, "we're coming up in the car in August to visit you and see the camp and that dreadful Jeb or Job or Jib or whatever you call him, who smokes a corn-cob pipe—ugh!"

The last they saw of her was a girlish shrug of disgust at that strange personage out of the West about whom (largely for her benefit) Roy and others had circulated the most outlandish tales. Jeb Rushmore was already ensconced in the unfinished camp, and from the few letters which had come from him it was judged that his excursion east had not spoiled him. One of these missives had been addressed to *Mister John Temple* and must have been a refreshing variation from the routine mail which awaited Mr. Temple each morning at the big granite bank. It read:

"Thar's a crittur come here to paint names o' animiles on the cabin doors. I told him friendly sich wuzn't wanted, likewise no numbers. He see it were best ter go. Bein' you put up th' money I would say polite and likewise explain ez how the skins uv animiles is propper fur signs an' not numbers bein' ez cabins is not railroad cars."

This is a fair sample of the letters which were received by Mr. Temple, by Mr. Ellsworth, and even at National Scout Headquarters, which Jeb Rushmore called "the main ranch."

The idea of putting the skin of a silver fox, for instance, on the patrol's cabin instead of a painted caricature of that animal, took the boys by storm, and to them at least Jeb Rushmore became a very real character long before they ever met him. They felt that Jeb Rushmore had the right idea and they were thrilled at the tragic possibilities of that ominous sentence, "He see it were best to go."

The whole troop was down at the boathouse to see the boys off. Tom and Roy wore old khaki trousers and faded shirts which had seen service in many a rough hike; their scarred duffel bags bore unmistakable signs of hard usage, but Pee-wee was resplendent in his full regalia, with his monogram burned in a complicated design into the polished leather of his brand new duffel bag. His "trousseau," as the boys called it, was indeed as complete and accurate as was possible. Even the scout smile, which is not the least part of the scout make-up, was carried to a conspicuous extreme; he smiled all over; he was one vast smile.

"Don't fall off any mountains, Pee-wee."

"Be sure to take your smile off when you go to bed."

"If you get tired, you can jump on a train."

"Pee-wee, you look as if you were posing for animal crackers."

These were some of the flippant comments which were hurled at Pee-wee as the three, in Roy's canoe, glided from the float and up the river on the first stage of what was destined to be an adventurous journey.

The river, along whose lower reaches Bridgeboro was situated, had its source within a mile or two of the Hudson in the vicinity of Nyack. From the great city it was navigable by power craft as far as Bridgeboro and even above at full tide, but a mile or two above the boys' home town it narrowed to a mere creek, winding its erratic way through a beautiful country where intertwined and overarching boughs formed dim tunnels through which the canoeist passed with no sound but the swishing of his own paddle. The boys had never before canoed to the river's source, though it was one of the things they had always been meaning to do. It was a happy thought of Tom's to make it a part of their journey now and strike into the roads along the Hudson in that way.

"Oh, crinkums, I'm crazy to see Jeb Rushmore, aren't you?" said Pee-wee. "I never thought I'd have a chance to go like this, I sure didn't! I never thought you'd want me."

"We couldn't do without you, kiddo," said Roy, as he paddled. "We wouldn't have any luck—you're our lucky penny."

"Cracky, you could have knocked me down with a feather when I got that note. At first, I thought you must be jollying me—and even now it doesn't seem real."

The boys laughed. "Well, here you are, kiddo," said Roy, "so you see it's real enough."

Percy K. Fitzhugh

"Do you suppose we'll have any adventures?"

"Why, as the little boy said when he spilled the ink on the parlor carpet, 'that remains to be seen.' We won't side-step any, you can be sure of that."

"There may be danger awaiting us," said Pee-wee.

"Well, I only hope it'll wait till we get to it," Roy laughed. "What do you say, kiddo, shall we hit it up for Nyack to-night or camp along the river?"

They decided to paddle leisurely, ending their canoe trip next day. About dusk they made their camp on a steep, wooded shore, and with the flame of their campfire reflected in the rippling water, Roy cooked supper.

Pee-wee was supremely happy. It is doubtful if he had ever before been so happy.

"There's one thing," said Tom, as he held the bacon over the flame. "I'm going to do my first-class stunts before we get there."

"And I'm going to do some tracking," said Roy; "here you go, Pee-wee, here's a bacon sandwich—look out for the juice. This is what Daniel Boone used to eat." He handed Pee-wee a sizzling slice of bacon between two cakes of sweet chocolate!

"Mmmmmmm," said Pee-wee, "that's scrumptious! Gee, I never knew chocolate and bacon went so good together."

"To-morrow for breakfast I'll give you a boiled egg stuffed with caraway seeds," said Roy.

"Give him a Dan Beard omelet," said Tom.

"What's that?" asked Pee-wee, his two hands and his mouth running with greasy chocolate.

"Salt codfish with whipped cream," answered Roy. "Think you'd like it?"

Pee-wee felt sure he would.

"And there's one thing *I'm* going to do," he said. "Tom's going to finish his first-class stunts and you're going to do tracking. I'm going to—"

"Have another sandwich?" interrupted Roy.

"Sure. And there's one thing I'm going to do. I'm going to test some good turns. Gee, there isn't room enough to test 'em indoors."

"Good for you," said Roy; "but you'd better trot down to the river now and wash your face. You look like the end man in a minstrel show. Then come on back and we'll reel off some campfire yarns."

They sat late into the night, until their fire burned low and Roy realized, as he had never before realized, what good company Pee-wee was. They slept as only those know how to sleep who go camping, and early in the morning continued their journey along the upper and tortuous reaches of the narrowing river.

Early in the spring there had been a serious flood which had done much damage even down in Bridgeboro, and the three boys as they paddled carefully along were surprised at the havoc which had been wrought here on the upper river.

Percy K. Fitzhugh

Small buildings along the shore lay toppled over, boats were here and there marooned high and dry many yards from the shore, and the river was almost impassable in places from the obstructions of uprooted trees and other debris.

At about noon they reached a point where the stream petered out so that further navigation even by canoe was impossible; but they were already in the outskirts of West Nyack.

"The next number on the program," said Roy, "is to administer first aid to the canoe in the form of a burlap bandage. Pee-wee, you're appointed chairman of the grass committee —pick some grass and let's pad her up."

If you have never administered "first aid" to a canoe and "padded it up" for shipment, let me tell you that the scout way of doing it is to bind burlap loosely around it and to stuff this with grass or hay so that the iron hook which is so gently wielded by the expressman may not damage the hull.

Having thus prepared it for its more prosaic return journey by train, they left the boat on the shore and following a beaten path came presently into the very heart of the thriving metropolis of West Nyack.

"I feel as if we were Lewis and Clarke, or somebody, arriving at an Indian village," said Pee-wee.

At the express office Roy arranged for the shipment of the canoe back to Bridgeboro, and then they started along the road toward Nyack. It was on this part of their journey that something happened which was destined materially to alter their program.

They had come into the main street of the village and were heading for the road which led to the Hudson when they came upon a little group of people looking amusedly up into an elm tree on the lawn of a stately residence. A little girl was standing beneath the tree in evident distress, occasionally wringing her hands as she looked fearfully up into the branches. Whatever was happening there was no joke to her, however funny it might be to the other onlookers.

"What's the matter?" Tom asked.

"Bird up there," briefly answered the nearest bystander.

"She'll never get it," said another.

"Oh, now he's going away," cried the little girl in despair.

The contrast between her anxiety and the amusement of the others was marked. Every time she called to the bird it flitted to another limb, and every time the bird flitted she wrung her hands and cried. An empty cage upon a lawn bench told the story.

"What's the matter?" said Pee-wee, going to the child and seeking his information first-hand.

"Oh, I'll never get him," she sobbed. "He'll fly away in a minute and I'll never see him again."

Pee-wee looked up into the branches and after some difficulty succeeded in locating a little bird somewhat smaller than a robin and as green as the foliage amid which it was so heedlessly disporting.

"I see him," said Pee-wee. "Gee, don't you cry; we'll get him some way. We're scouts, we are, and we'll get him for you."

His reassuring words did not seem to comfort the girl. "Oh,

Percy K. Fitzhugh

there he goes!" she cried. "Now he's going to fly away!"

He did not fly away but merely flew to another limb and began to preen himself. For so small a bird he was attracting a great deal of notice in the world. Following Pee-wee's lead, others including Tom and Roy ventured upon the lawn, smiling and straining their eyes to follow the tantalizing movements of the little fugitive.

"Of course," said Pee-wee to the girl, "it would be easy enough to shin up that tree—that would be a cinch— anybody could do that—I mean any *feller*—of course, a girl couldn't; but I'd only frighten him away."

"You'll never get him," said one man.

"What kind of a bird is it?" Tom asked.

"It's a dwarf parrot," the girl sobbed, "and I'll never get him —never!"

"You don't want to get discouraged," said Pee-wee. "Gee, there's always some way."

The spectators evidently did not agree with him. Some of them remained about, smiling; others went away. The diminutive Pee-wee seemed to amuse them quite as much as the diminutive parrot, but all were agreed (as they continually remarked to each other) that the bird was a "goner."

"Is he tame?" Roy asked.

"He was *getting* tame," the girl sobbed, "and he was learning to say my name. My father would give a hundred dollars— Oh," she broke off, "now he *is* going away!" She began to cry pitifully.

Pee-wee stood a moment thoughtfully. "Have you got a garden hose?" he presently asked.

"Yes, but you're not going to squirt water at him," said the girl, indignantly.

"If you get the garden hose," said Pee-wee, "I'll bring him down for you."

"What are you going to do, kiddo?" Roy asked.

"You'll see," said Pee-wee.

The other boys looked at each other, puzzled. The girl looked half incredulously at Pee-wee and something in his manner gave her a feeling of hope. Most of the others laughed good-humoredly.

They hauled the nozzle end of a garden hose from where it lay coiled near a faucet in the stone foundation. Pee-wee took the nozzle and began to play the stream against the trunk of the tree, all the while looking up at the parrot. Presently, the bird began to "sit up and take notice," as one might say. It was plainly interested. The bystanders began to "sit up and take notice" too, and they watched the bird intently as it cocked its head and listened. Pee-wee sent the stream a little higher up the trunk and as he did so the bird became greatly excited. It began uttering, in the modulated form consonant with its size, the discordant squawk of the parrot. The little girl watched eagerly.

"Get the cage," ordered Pee-wee.

Roy brought it and laid it at his feet. The stream played a little higher, and the bird chattered furiously and came lower.

"Remind you of home?" Pee-wee asked, looking up and playing the water a little higher. The bystanders watched, in silence. The bird was now upon the lowest branch, chattering like mad and flapping its wings frantically. The little girl, in an ecstasy of fresh hope, called to it and danced up and down.

But Pee-wee, like a true artist, neither saw nor heard his audience. He was playing the bird with this line of water as an angler plays a fish. And never was moth lured by a flame more irresistibly than this little green fugitive was lured by the splashing of that stream.

"Oh, can you catch him? Can you catch him?" pleaded the girl as she clutched Pee-wee's arm.

"Let go a minute," said Pee-wee. "Now, all stand back, here goes!"

He shot the stream suddenly down at the base of the tree, holding the nozzle close so that the plashing was loud and the spray diffused. And as an arrow goes to its mark the bird came swooping down plunk into the middle of the spray and puddle. Still playing the stream with one hand, Pee-wee reached carefully and with his other gently encircled the little drenched body.

"Quite an adventure, wasn't it, Greenie?" he said. "Where'd you think you were? In the tropics?— If you ever want to take hold of a bird," he added, turning to the girl, "hold it this way; make a ring out of your thumb and first finger, and let his stomach rest on the palm of your hand. Be sure your hand isn't cold, though. Here you are—that's right."

The girl could hardly speak. She stood with her dwarf parrot in her hand, looking at the stream of water which was now shooting silently through the grass and at the puddle which it had made, and she felt that a miracle had been performed before her eyes. Roy, hardly less pleased than she, stepped forward and turned off the water.

"Good work," said a gentleman. "I've seen many a bird brought down, but never in that fashion before."

"*We* don't use the other fashion," said Tom, with a touch of pride as he put his hand on Pee-wee's shoulder. "Do we, kid?"

"If it was a canary," said Pee-wee, "I might possibly have whistled him down, but not near enough to catch him, I guess. But as soon as I knew that bird came from the tropics, I knew he'd fall for water, 'cause a tropical bird'll go where the sound of water is every time. I guess it's because they have so many showers down there, or something. Then once I heard that it's best to turn on the faucet when you're teaching a parrot to talk. It's the sound of water. Did you get any water on you?" he asked, suddenly turning to the child.

There was no water on her clothing, but there was some in her eyes.

"I—I—think you're wonderful," she said. "I think you are just wonderful!"

"'Twasn't me," said Pee-wee, "it was the water. Gee," he added confidentially, "I often said I hated water, and I do hate a rainy day. And if you get any water in a carburetor— *goo-od-night*! But I got to admit water's good for some things."

"Oh, I want you please to wait—just a few minutes—I want to go and speak to my father," the girl said, as the boys started to move away. They were the only ones left now. "Please wait just a minute."

"We're on our way to Nyack," said Roy, suspecting her intention, "and I'm afraid we've lost as much time as we dare. We've got to do a little shopping there and our weather prophet here thinks we're going to have a *real* tropical shower before long."

"But won't you let my father give you each—something? You've been so good and it's—oh—it's just *wonderful*!"

"Pee-wee, you're the doctor," said Roy.

"I got to do a good turn every day," said the "doctor," "because we're scouts and that's the rule. If we took anything for it, why, then it wouldn't be a good turn. It would spoil all the fun. We're going on a long hike, up the Hudson to our camp. We don't want to go near railroad trains—and things like that. These fellows are taking me with them; that's a good turn, but if somebody paid 'em to do it, it wouldn't be a good turn, would it? I'm thankful to you and your parrot that you gave me the chance. Now I don't have to think of a good turn again till tomorrow. Besides I just happened to know about parrots and water so it's no credit to me."

That was it—he just happened to know! It was one of the dozens of things that he "just happened to know." How he came by the knowledge was a mystery. But perhaps the best thing he knew was that a service is a service and that you knock it in the head as soon as you take payment for it.

The girl watched them, as they jumped the hedge, laughing gaily at Pee-wee's clumsiness and, waving their hats to her, took their belated way along the road.

It was not the most popular way of bringing down a bird, but there was no blood on Pee-wee's hands, and it was a pretty good stunt at that!

CHAPTER VI

THE SHELTER

"Pee-wee, you're a wonder," said Roy. "You're the only original Boy Scout; how did you get next to that stunt? What do you think of him, Tom?"

"Some wrinkle," said Tom.

"Crinkums!" said Pee-wee. "I'm mighty glad I got him. If it hadn't succeeded I'd have felt cheap, sure; but when you're dealing with a girl, you always want to act as if you're sure of yourself. Do you know why?"

"Can't imagine," said Roy. "Break it to us gently."

"Because girls are never sure of themselves and they'll never take much stock in what you say unless you seem to be sure of yourself. That's one thing I've noticed. I've made a study of girls, kind of—And you're more apt to succeed if there's a girl watching you—did you ever notice that?"

Roy laughed.

"It's so," urged Pee-wee. "And there's another thing about girls, too; they're repulsive."

"What?" said Tom.

"*What?*" said Roy.

"They say the first thing that comes into their heads."

"*Im*pulsive, you mean," laughed Roy.

"Well, they're all right on good turns," said Tom.

"They don't have any good turns in the Camp Fire Girls," said Pee-wee.

"A girl might do a good turn and you'd never know anything about it," said Tom, significantly.

"Cracky," said Pee-wee, "she was tickled to get that bird back."

In a little while they were tramping along the main street of Nyack, heading for the lordly Hudson. It was almost twilight, the shops were shutting their doors, and as they came around the hill which brought them face to face with the river, the first crimson glow of sunset fell upon the rippling current. Across the wide expanse, which seemed the wider for the little winding stream they had so lately followed, the hills were already turning from green to gray and tiny lights were visible upon the rugged heights. A great white steamer with its light already burning was plowing majestically upstream and the little open craft at the shore rocked in the diminishing ripples which it sent across the water, as though bowing in humble obeisance to it.

"Gee, it's lonely, isn't it!" said Pee-wee.

"Not getting homesick, are you, kiddo?"

"No, but it seems kind of lonesome. I'm glad there's three of us. Oh, jiminy, look at those hills."

The scene was indeed such as to make the mightiest man feel insignificant.

The map showed a road which led to Haverstraw, and this the boys decided to follow until they should find a convenient spot in which to bivouac for the night. It followed the Hudson, sometimes running along the very brink with the mighty highlands rising above it and sometimes running between hills which shut the river from their view.

"Hark," said Tom. "What did I tell you! Thunder!"

A low, distant rumble sounded, and as they paused in the gathering darkness, listening, a little fitful gust blew Pee-wee's hat off.

"We're going to get a good dose of it," said Tom. "I've been smelling it for the last hour; look at those trees."

The leaves were blowing this way and that.

"We should worry," said Roy. "Didn't I tell you we might have to get our feet wet? This is a risky bus—"

"Shut up!" said Pee-wee.

They had walked not more than a quarter of a mile more when they came upon a stretch of road which was very muddy, with a piece of lowland bordering it. It was too dark to see clearly, but in the last remnant of daylight the boys could just distinguish a small, peculiar looking structure in the middle of this vast area.

"That's a funny place to build a house," said Roy.

"Maybe it's a fisherman's shack," Tom suggested.

Whatever it was, it was a most isolated and lonesome habitation, standing in the centre of that desert flat, shut in by the precipitous hills.

"It would be a good place for a hermit," said Roy. "You don't suppose anyone lives there, do you?"

"Cracky, wouldn't you like to be a hermit! Do you know what I'd like to have now—"

"An umbrella," interrupted Tom.

The remark, notwithstanding that it shocked Pee-wee's sense of fitness, inasmuch as they were scouting and "roughing it," was not inappropriate, for even as Tom spoke the patter of great drops was heard.

"Maybe it's been raining here this afternoon," observed Tom, "and that's what makes all this mud."

"Well, it's certainly raining here now," said Roy. "Me for that shack!"

The rain suddenly came down in torrents and the boys turned up their collars and made a dash across the marshy land toward the shadowy structure. Roy reached it first and, turning, called: "Hey, fellows, it's a boat!"

The others, drenched, but laughing, followed him, scrambling upon the deck and over the combing into the cockpit of a dilapidated cabin launch.

"What do you know about that!" said Roy. "Strike a light and let's see where we're at. I feel like a wet dish rag."

Presently Pee-wee's flashlight was poking its bright shaft this way and that as they looked curiously about them. They were in a neglected and disheveled, but very cosy, little cabin with sleeping lockers on either side and chintz curtains at the tiny portholes. A two-cylinder engine, so rusted that the wheel wouldn't turn over and otherwise in a dubious condition, was ineffectually covered by a piece of stiff and rotten oil cloth, the floor was cluttered with junk, industrious spiders had woven their webs all about and a frantic scurrying sound told of the hurried departure of some little animal which had evidently made its home in the forsaken hull.

"Oh, but this is great!" enthused Pee-wee. "This is the kind of an adventure you read about; *now* our adventures have really started."

"It'll be more to the purpose if we can get our supper really started," said Roy.

"How do you suppose it got here?" Pee-wee asked.

"That's easy," said Tom. "I didn't realize it before, but the tide must come up over the road sometimes and flood all this land here. That's what makes the road muddy. There must have been a good high tide some time or other, and it brought the boat right up over the road and here it is, marooned."

"Maybe it was the same flood that did all the damage down our way," Roy said. "Well, here goes; get the things out, Pee-wee, and we'll have some eats. Gee, it's nice in here."

It *was* nice. The rain pattered down on the low roof and beat against the little ports; the boat swayed a little in the heavier gusts of wind and all the delightful accompaniments of a life on the ocean wave were present—except the peril.

"You get out the cooking things," said Roy, "while I take a squint around and see if I can find something to kindle a fire in."

He did not have to go far. Sliding open the little hatch, he emerged into the cockpit, where the wind and rain smote him mercilessly. The storm had grown into a tempest and Roy wondered how it would be out on the wide river on such a night. In the cockpit was nothing but the shredded remnant of a sun awning and a couple of camp chairs, but a few feet from the boat something on the mushy ground cast a faint glimmer, and on going to it he found it to be a battered five-gallon gasoline can, which he brought back in triumph. By this time Tom and Pee-wee had the camp lamp burning and the supper things laid out. It was a very cosy scene.

"See if there's a Stillson wrench in that locker," said Roy.

Among the rusted tools was a "Stillson," and with this Roy disconnected the exhaust pipe from the engine. He next partly "jabbed" and partly cut a hole in the gasoline can of about the circumference of the pipe. A larger hole in the side of the can sufficed for a door and he squeezed the end of the exhaust pipe into the hole he had made for it, and presto! there was a very serviceable makeshift stove with the exhaust system of the engine converted into a draught and chimney.

"The new patent Silver Fox cooking stove," said Roy. "A scout is resourceful. This beats trying to kindle a fire outside, a night like this. Chuck that piece of wood over here."

Percy K. Fitzhugh

There was an old battery box knocking about and this Roy whittled into shavings, while the others with their belt axes completed the ruin of the awning stanchions by chopping them into pieces a few inches long.

"Guess they weren't good for much," observed Tom.

"Oh," said Pee-wee, "I'd just like to live in this boat."

It was no wonder he felt so. With the fire burning brightly in the old can and sending its smoke out through the boat's exhaust, the smell of the bacon cooking, the sight of their outer garments drying in the cheery warmth, while the wind howled outside and the rain beat down upon the low roof the situation was not half bad and an occasional lurch of the old hull gave a peculiar charm to their odd refuge.

"Could you dally with a rice cake, kiddo?" asked Roy, as he deftly stirred up some rice and batter. "Sling me that egg powder, Tom, and give me something to stir with—not that, you gump, that's the fever thermometer!"

"Here's a fountain pen," said Pee-wee; "will that do?"

"This screw-driver will be better," said Roy. "Here, kiddo, make yourself useful and keep turning that in the pan. You're a specialist on good turns."

Pee-wee stirred, while Tom attended to the fire, and Roy to the cooking. And I might mention on the side that if you should happen to be marooned in a disused boat on a blustering night, and are ingenious enough (as Roy was) to contrive the cooking facilities, you cannot do better than flop a few rice cakes, watching carefully that they don't burn. You can flop them with a shoe horn if you've nothing better at hand.

They spread their balloon silk tent in the cockpit, holding fast to the corners until enough water had fallen into it to fill the coffee-pot, and they had three such cups of coffee as you never fancied in your fondest dreams.

For dessert they had "Silver Fox Slump," an invention of Roy's made with chocolate, honey and, I think, horse-radish. It has to be stirred thoroughly. Pee-wee declared that it was such a *table d'hote* dinner as he had never before tasted. He was always partial to the scout style of cooking and he added, "You know how they have music at *table d'hote* dinners. Well, this music's got it beat, that's one sure thing. Gee, I'll hate to leave the boat, I sure will."

The boisterous music gave very little prospect of ceasing, and after the three had talked for an hour or so, they settled down for the night, two on the lockers and one on the floor, with the wind still moaning and the rain coming down in torrents.

When they awoke in the morning the wind had died down somewhat, but it still blew fitfully out of the east and the rain had settled down into a steady drizzle. Tom ventured out into the cockpit and looked about him. The hills across the river were gray in the mist and the wide expanse of water was steel color. He could see now that there was another road close under the precipitous cliffs and that the one which divided this lowland from the river was almost awash. Through the mist and drizzle along this higher road came a man. He left the road and started to pick his way across the flat, hailing as he came. The three boys awaited him in the cockpit.

"Don't nobody leave that boat!" he called, "or I'll shoot."

"Dearie me," said Roy. "He seems to be peeved. What are

we up against, anyway?"

"Don't shoot, mister," called Tom. "You couldn't drag us out of here with a team of horses."

"Tell him we are Boy Scouts and fear naught," whispered Pee-wee. "Tell him we scorn his—er—what d'you call it?"

"Hey, mister," called Roy. "We are Boy Scouts and fear naught, and we scorn your what-d'you-call it."

"Haouw?" called the man.

"What's that he's got on?" said Tom, "a merit badge?"

"It's a cop's badge," whispered Pee-wee. "Oh, crinkums, we're pinched."

The man approached, dripping and breathing heavily, and placed his hands on the combing.

"Anybody here 'sides you youngsters?" he demanded, at the same time peering inside the cabin.

"A few spiders," said Tom.

"Whatcher doin' here, anyway?"

"We're waiting for the storm to hold up," said Roy; "we beat it from that road when—"

"We sought refuge," Pee-wee prompted him.

"Any port in a storm, you know," Roy smiled. "Are we pinched?"

The man did not vouchsafe an immediate answer to this vital query. Instead he poked his head in, peered about and then said, "Don' know's ye are, not fur's I'm concerned. I'd like to hev ye answer me one question honest, though."

"You'll have to answer one for us first," called Roy, who had disappeared within the little cabin. "Do you take two lumps of sugar in your coffee?"

The man now condescended to smile, as Roy brought out a steaming cup and handed it to him.

"Wall, ye've got all the comforts uv home, ain't ye?"

"Give him a rice cake," whispered Pee-wee in Roy's ear. "He's all right."

"Won't you come in?" said Roy. "I don't know whose boat this is, but you're welcome. I guess we didn't do any damage. We chopped up a couple of broken stanchions, that's all."

"I guess we'll let ye off without more'n ten year uv hard labor," said the man, sipping his coffee. "But I'll give ye a tip. Get away from here as soon's ye can,—hear? Old man Stanton owns this boat an' he's a bear. He'd run ye in fer trespass and choppin' up them stanchions quick as a gun. Ye come oft'n that outer road, ye say? Strangers here?"

"I can see now that road is flooded," said Tom. "Guess it isn't used, is it?"

"This is all river land," said the man. "In extra high tides this here land is flooded an' the only ones usin' that thar road is the fishes. This rain keeps up another couple of days an' we get a full moon on top o' that the old hulk'll float, by gol! Ye didn't see no men around here last night now, did ye?"

"Not a soul," said Roy.

"'Cause there was a prisoner escaped up yonder last night an' when I see the smoke comin' out o' yer flue contraption here I thought like enough he hit this shelter."

"Up yonder?" Tom queried.

"You're strangers, hey?" the man repeated.

"We're on a hike," said Tom. "We're on our way to Haverstraw and—"

"Thence," prompted Pee-wee.

"*Thence* to Catskill Landing, and *thence* to Leeds and *thence* to Black Lake," mocked Roy.

"Well, thar's a big prison up yonder," said the man.

"Oh, Sing Sing?" Roy asked. "I never thought of that."

"Feller scaled the wall last night an' made off in a boat."

The boys were silent. They had not realized how close they were to Ossining, and the thought of the great prison whose name they had often heard mentioned sobered them a little; the mere suggestion of one of its inmates scaling its frowning wall on such a night and setting forth in an open boat, perhaps lurking near their very shelter, cast a shadow over them.

"Are you—are you *sure* you didn't see a—a crouching shadow when you went out and got that gasoline can last night?" Pee-wee stammered.

"I'm sorry," said Roy, "but I didn't see one crouching shadow."

"His boat might have upset in the storm," Tom suggested. "The wind even shook this boat; it must have been pretty rough out on the river."

"Like enough," said the man. "Des'pret characters'll take des'pret chances."

"What did he do?" Pee-wee asked, his imagination thoroughly aroused.

"Dunno," said the man. "Burglary, like enough. Well now, you youngsters have had yer shelter'n the wust o' the storm's over. It's goin' ter keep right on steady like this till after full moon, an' the ole shebang'll be floppin' roun' the marsh like enough on full moon tide. My advice to you is to git along. Not that you done no damage or what *I'd* call damage—but it won't do no good fer yer to run amuck o' Ole Man Stanton. 'Cause he's a reg'lar grizzly, as the feller says."

The boys were silent a moment. Perhaps the thought of that desperate convict stealing forth amid the wind and rain still gripped them; but it began to dawn upon them also that they had been trespassing and that they had taken great liberties with this ramshackle boat.

That the owner could object to their use of it seemed preposterous. That he could take advantage of the technical "damage" done was quite unsupposable. But no one knows better than a boy how many "grouchy" men there are in the world, and these very boys had once been ordered out of John Temple's lot with threat and menace.

"Does *everybody* call him 'Old Man' Stanton?" Pee-wee

asked. "Because if they do that's pretty bad. Whenever somebody is known as 'Old Man' it sounds pretty bad for him. They used to say 'Old Man Temple'—he's a man we know that owns a lot of railroads and things; of course, he's reformed now—he's a magnet—"

"Magnate," corrected Roy.

"But they *used* to call him 'Old Man Temple'—everybody did. And it's a sure sign—you can always tell," Pee-wee concluded.

"Wall, they call *me* 'Ole Man Flint,'" said the visitor, "so I guess—"

"Oh, of course," said Pee-wee, hastily, "I don't say it's always so, and besides you're a—a—"

"Sheriff," Mr. Flint volunteered.

"So you got to be kind of strict—and—and grouchy—like."

The sheriff handed his empty cup to Roy and smiled good-naturedly.

"Where does Old Man Stanton live?" asked Tom, who had been silent while the others were talking.

"'Long the Nyack road, but he has his office in Nyack—he's a lawyer," said the visitor, as he drew his rubber hat down over his ears.

"Can we get back to Nyack by that other road?"

"Whatcher goin' to do?"

"We'll have to go and see Old Man Stanton," Tom said, "then if we don't get pinched we'll start north."

Mr. Flint looked at him in astonishment.

"I wouldn't say we've done any damage," said Tom in his stolid way, "and I believe in that about any port in a storm. But if he's the kind of a man who would think different, then we've got to go and tell him, that's all. We can pay him for the stanchions we chopped up."

"Wall, you're a crazy youngster, that's all, but if yer sot on huntin' fer trouble, yer got only yerself to blame. Ye'll go before a justice uv the peace, the whole three uv year, and be fined ten dollars apiece, likely as not, an' I don't believe ye've got twenty-five dollars between the lot uv yer."

"Right you are," said Roy. "We are poor but honest, and we spurn—don't we, Pee-wee?"

"Sure we do," agreed Pee-wee.

"Poverty is no disgrace," said Roy dramatically.

The man, though not overburdened with a sense of humor, could not help smiling at Roy and he went away laughing, but scarcely crediting their purpose to venture into the den of "Old Man Stanton." "They're a queer lot," he said to himself.

Within a few minutes the boys had gathered up their belongings, repacked their duffel bags and were picking their way across the marsh toward the drier road.

"We're likely to land in jail," said Pee-wee, mildly protesting.

"It isn't a question of whether we land in jail or not," said Tom, stolidly; "it's just a question of what we ought to do."

"*We* should worry," said Roy.

CHAPTER VII

THE "GOOD TURN"

It was a draggled and exceedingly dubious-looking trio that made their way up the main street of Nyack. They had no difficulty in finding the office of "Old Man Stanton," which bore a conspicuous sign:

WILMOUTH STANTON
COUNSELLOR AT LAW

"He'd—he'd have to get out a warrant for us first, wouldn't he?" Pee-wee asked, apprehensively.

"That'll be easy," said Roy. "If all goes well, I don't see why we shouldn't be in Sing Sing by three o'clock."

"We're big fools to do this," said Pee-wee. "A scout is supposed to be—cautious." But he followed the others up the stairs and stepped bravely in when Tom opened the door.

They found themselves in the lion's den with the lion in close proximity glaring upon them. He sat at a desk opening mail and looked frowningly at them over his spectacles. He was thin and wiry, his gray hair was rumpled in a way which suggested perpetual perplexity or annoyance, and his general

Percy K. Fitzhugh

aspect could not be said to be either conciliatory or inviting.

"Well, sir," he said, crisply.

"Are you Mr. Stanton?" Tom asked. "We are Scouts," he added, as the gentleman nodded perfunctorily, "and we came from Bridgeboro. We're on our way to camp. Last night we got caught in the rain and we ran—"

"Took refuge," whispered Pee-wee.

"For that old boat on the marsh. This morning we heard it was yours, so we came to tell you that we camped in it last night. We made a fire in a can, but I don't think we did any harm, except we chopped up a couple of old stanchions. We thought they were no good, but, of course, we shouldn't have taken them without leave."

Mr. Stanton stared at him with an ominous frown. "Built a fire in a can?" said he. "Do you mean in the boat?"

"We used the exhaust for a draught," said Roy.

"Oh—and what brings you here?"

"To tell you," said Tom, doggedly. "A man came and told us you owned the boat. He said you might have us arrested, so we came to let you know about what we did."

"We didn't come because we wanted to be arrested," put in Pee-wee.

"I see," said Mr. Stanton, with the faintest suggestion of a smile. "Isn't it something new," he added, "running into the jaws of death? Boys generally run the other way and don't go hunting for trouble."

"Well, I'll tell you how it is," said Pee-wee, making the conversation his own, somewhat to Roy's amusement. "Of course, a scout has got to be cautious—but he's got to be fearless too. I was kind of scared when I heard you were a lawyer—"

Mr. Stanton's grim visage relaxed into an unwilling, but unmistakable, smile.

"And another thing I heard scared me, but—"

Tom, seeing where Pee-wee was drifting, tried to stop him, but Roy, knowing that Pee-wee always managed to land on top, and seeing the smile on Mr. Stanton's forbidding countenance, encouraged him to go on, and presently the mascot of the Silver Foxes was holding the floor.

"A scout has to deduce—that's one of the things we learn, and if you heard somebody called 'Old Man Something-or-other,' why, you'd deduce something from it, wouldn't you? And you'd be kind of scared-like. But even if you deduce that a man is going to be mad and gruff, kind of, even still you got to remember that you're a scout and if you damaged his property you got to go and tell him, anyway. You got to go and tell him even if you go to jail. Don't you see? Maybe you don't know much about the scouts—"

"No," said Mr. Stanton, "I'm afraid I don't. But I'm glad to know that I am honored by a nickname—even so dubious a one. Do you think you were correct in your deductions?" he added.

"Well, I don't know," began Pee-wee. "I can see—well, anyway there's another good thing about a scout—he's got to admit it if he's wrong."

Mr. Stanton laughed outright. It was a rusty sort of laugh, for he did not laugh often—but he laughed.

"The only things I know about Boy Scouts," said he, "I have learned in the last twenty-four hours. You tell me that they can convert an exhaust pipe into a stove flue, and I have learned they can bring a bird down out of a tree without so much as a bullet or a stone (I have to believe what my little daughter tells me), and that they take the road where they think trouble awaits them on account of a principle—that they walk up to the cannon's mouth, as it were—I am a very busy man and no doubt a very hard and disagreeable one, but I can afford to know a little more about these scouts, I believe."

"I'll tell you all about them," said Pee-wee, sociably. "Jiminys, I never dreamed you were that girl's father."

Mr. Stanton swung around in his chair and looked at him sharply. "Who are you boys?"

"We came from Bridgeboro in New Jersey," spoke up Roy, "and we're going up the river roads as far as Catskill Landing. Then we're going to hit inland for our summer camp."

Mr. Stanton was silent for a few moments, looking keenly at them while they stood in some suspense.

"Well," he said, soberly, "I see but one way out of the difficulty. The stanchions you destroyed were a part of the boat. The boat is of no use to me without them. I suggest, therefore, that you take the boat along with you. It belonged to my son and it has been where it now lies ever since the storm in which his life was lost. I have not seen the inside of it since—I do not want to see the inside of it," he added brusquely, moving a paperweight about on his desk. "It is only three years old," he went on after a moment's uncomfortable pause, "and like some people it is not as bad as it looks."

The boys winced a little at this thrust. Mr. Stanton was silent for a few moments and Pee-wee was tempted to ask him something about his son, but did not quite dare to venture.

"I think the boat can very easily be removed to the river with a little of the ingenuity which you scouts seem to have, and you may continue your journey in her, if you care to. You may consider it a—a present from my daughter, whom you made so happy yesterday."

For a moment the boys hardly realized the meaning of his words. Then Tom spoke.

"We have a rule, Mr. Stanton, that a scout cannot accept anything for a service. If he does, it spoils it all. It's great, your offering us the boat and it seems silly not to take it, but—"

"Very well," said Mr. Stanton, proceeding to open his letters, "if you prefer to go to jail for destroying my stanchions, very well. Remember you are dealing with a lawyer." Roy fancied he was chuckling a little inwardly.

"That's right," said Pee-wee in Tom's ear. "There's no use trying to get the best of a lawyer—a scout ought to be—to be modest; we better take it, Tom."

"There's a difference between payment for a service and a token of gratitude," said Mr. Stanton, looking at Tom. "But we will waive all that. I cannot allow the Boy Scouts to be laying down the law for me. By your own confession you have destroyed my stanchions and as a citizen it is my duty to take action. But if I were to give you a paper dated yesterday, assigning the boat to you, then it would appear that you had simply trespassed and burglariously entered your own property and destroyed your own stanchions and I would not have a leg to stand upon. My advice to you as a lawyer is to accept such a transfer of title and avoid trouble."

He began ostentatiously to read one of his letters.

"He's right, Tom," whispered Pee-wee, "It's what you call a teckinality. Gee, we better take the boat. There's no use trying to beat a lawyer. He's got the right on his side."

"I don't know," said Tom, doubtfully. He, too, fancied that Mr. Stanton was laughing inwardly, but he was not good at repartee and the lawyer was too much for him. It was Roy who took the situation in hand.

"It seems ungrateful, Mr. Stanton, even to talk about whether we'll take such a peach of a gift. Tom here is always thinking about the law—our law—and Pee-wee—we call this kid Pee-wee—he's our specialist on doing good turns. They're both cranks in different ways. I know there's a difference, as you say, between just a present and a reward. And it seems silly to say thank you for such a present, just as if it was a penknife or something like that. But we do thank you and we'll take the boat. I just happened to think of a good name for it while you were talking. It was the good turn Pee-wee did yesterday—about the bird, I mean—that made you offer it to us and your giving it to us is a good turn besides, so I guess we'll call it the 'Good Turn.'"

"You might call it the 'Teckinality,'" suggested Mr. Stanton with a glance at Pee-wee.

"All right," he added, "I'll send one of my men down later in the day to see about getting her in the water. I've an idea a block and falls will do the trick. But you'd better caulk her up with lampwick and give her a coat of paint in the meantime."

He went to the door with them and as they turned at the foot of the stairs and called back another "Thank you," Roy noticed something in his face which had not been there before.

"I bet he's thinking of his son," said he.

"Wonder how he died," said Tom.

CHAPTER VIII

BON VOYAGE!

"Now, you see," said Pee-wee, "how a good turn can evolute."

"Can what?" said Tom.

"Evolute."

"It could neverlute with me," observed Roy. "Gee, but we've fallen in soft! You could have knocked me down with a toothpick. I wonder what our sleuth friend, the sheriff, will say."

The sheriff said very little; he was too astonished to say much. So were most of the people of the town. When they heard that "Old Man Stanton" had given Harry Stanton's boat to some strange boys from out of town, they said that the loss of his son must have affected his mind. The boys of the neighborhood, incredulous, went out on the marsh the next day when the rain held up, and stood about watching the three strangers at work and marvelling at "Old Man Stanton's" extraordinary generosity.

"Aw, he handed 'em a lemon!" commented the wiseacre.

"That boat'll never run—it won't even float!"

But Harry Stanton's cruising launch was no lemon. It proved to be staunch and solid. There wasn't a rotten plank in her. Her sorry appearance was merely the superficial shabbiness which comes from disuse and this the boys had neither the time nor the money to remedy; but the hull and the engine were good.

To the latter Roy devoted himself, for he knew something of gas engines by reason of the two automobiles at his own house. They made a list of the things they needed, took another hike into Nyack and came back laden with material and provisions. Roy poured a half-gallon or so of kerosene into each of the two cylinders and left it over night. The next morning when he drained it off the wheel turned over easily enough. A set of eight dry cells, some new wiring, a couple of new plugs, a little session with a pitted coil, a little more gas, a little less air, a little more gas, and finally the welcome first explosion, so dear to the heart of the motor-boatist, rewarded Roy's efforts of half a day.

"Stop it! Stop it!" shrieked Pee-wee from outside. "I hung the paint can on the propeller! I'm getting a green shower bath!"

He poked his head over the combing, his face, arms and clothing bespattered with copper paint.

"Never mind, kiddo," laughed Roy, "It's all in the game. She runs like a dream. Step a little closer, ladies and gentlemen, and view the leopard boy. Pee-wee, you're a sight! For goodness' sakes, get some sandpaper!"

The two days of working on the *Good Turn* were two days of fun. It was not necessary to caulk her lower seams for the dampness of the marsh had kept them tight, and the seams above were easy. They did not bother about following the water-line and painting her free-board white; a coat of copper paint over the whole hull sufficed. They painted the sheathing of the cockpit a common-sense brown, "neat but not gaudy," as Roy said. The deck received a coat of an unknown color which their friend, the sheriff, brought them saying he had used it on his chicken-coop. The engine they did in aluminum paint, the fly-wheel in a gaudy red, and then they mixed what was left of all the paints.

"I bet we get a kind of blackish white," said Pee-wee.

"I bet it's green," said Tom.

But it turned out to be a weak silvery gray and with this they painted the cabin, or rather half the cabin, for their paint gave out.

They sat until long after midnight in the little cabin after their first day's work, but were up and at it again bright and early in the morning, for Mr. Stanton's men were coming with the block and falls at high tide in the evening to haul the *Good Turn* back into her watery home.

Pee-wee spent a good part of the day throwing out superfluous junk and tidying up the little cabin, while Tom and Roy repaired the rubbing-rail where it had broken loose and attended to other slight repairs on the outside.

The dying sunlight was beginning to flicker on the river and the three were finishing their supper in the cabin when Tom, looking through the porthole, called, "Oh, here comes the truck and an automobile just in front of it!"

Sure enough, there on the road was the truck with its great coil of hempen rope and its big pulleys, accompanied by two men in overalls. Pee-wee could not repress his exuberance as the trio clambered up on the cabin roof and waved to the little cavalcade.

"In an hour more she'll be in the water," he shouted, "and we'll—"

"We'll anchor till daylight," concluded Roy.

In another moment a young girl, laden with bundles, had left the automobile and was picking her way across the marsh. It proved to be the owner of the fugitive bird.

"I've brought you all the things that belong to the boat," she said, "and I'm going to stay and see it launched. My father was coming too but he had a meeting or something or other. Isn't it perfectly glorious how you chopped up the stanchions—"

"Great," said Roy. "It shows the good that comes out of breaking the law. If we hadn't chopped up the stanchions—"

"Oh, crinkums, look at this!" interrupted Pee-wee. He was handling the colored bow lamp.

"And here's the compass, and here's the whistle, and here's the fog-bell," said the girl, unloading her burden with a sigh of relief. "And here's the flag for the stern and here—look—I made this all by myself and sat up till eleven o'clock to do it—see!"

She unfolded a cheese-cloth pennant with the name *Good Turn* sewed upon it. "You have to fly this at the bow in memory of your getting my bird for me," she said.

"We'll fly it at the bow in memory of what you and your

Percy K. Fitzhugh

father have done for *us*," said Tom.

"And here's some fruit, and here's some salmon, and here's some pickled something or other—I got them all out of the pantry and they weigh a ton!"

There was no time for talking if the boat was to be got to the river before dark, and the boys fell to with the men while the girl looked about the cabin with exclamations of surprise.

"Isn't it perfectly lovely," she called to Tom, who was outside encircling the hull with a double line of heavy rope, under the men's direction. "I never saw anything so cute and wasn't it a fine idea giving it to you!"

"Bully," said Tom.

"It was just going to ruin here," she said, "and it was a shame."

It was a busy scene that followed and the boys had a glimpse of the wonderful power of the block and falls. To an enormous tree on the roadside a gigantic three-wheel pulley was fastened by means of a metal band around the lower part of the trunk. Several other pulleys between this and the boat multiplied the hauling power to such a degree that one person pulling on the loose end which was left after the rope had been passed back and forth many times through the several pulleys, could actually move the boat. The hull was completely encircled, the rope running along the sides and around the stern with another rope below near the keel so that the least amount of strain would be put upon her.

They hitched the horses to the rope's end and as the beasts plunged through the yielding marsh the boat came reeling and lurching toward the road. Here they laid planks and rollers and jacked her across. This was not so much a matter of brute strength as of skill. The two men with the aid of the Stanton chauffeur were able, with props of the right length, to keep the *Good Turn* on an even keel, while the boys removed and replaced the rollers. It was interesting to see how the bulky hull could be moved several hundred feet, guided and urged across a road and retarded upon the down grade to the river by two or three men who knew just how to do it.

Cautiously the rollers were retarded with obstructing sticks, as the men, balancing the hull upright, let her slowly down the slope into the water. Pee-wee stood upon the road holding the rope's end and a thrill went through him when he felt the rocking and bobbing of the boat as it regained its wonted home, and at last floated freely in the water.

"Hang on to that, youngster," called one of the men. "She's where she can do as she likes now."

As the *Good Turn*, free at last from prosaic rollers and plank tracks, rolled easily in the swell, pulling gently upon the rope which the excited Pee-wee held, it seemed that she must be as pleased as her new owners were, at finding herself once more in her natural home. How graceful and beautiful she looked now, in the dying light! There is nothing so clumsy looking as a boat on shore. To one who has seen a craft "laid up," it is hardly recognizable when launched.

"Well, there ye are," said one of the men, "an' 'tain't dark yet neither. You can move 'er by pullin' one finger now, hey? She looks mighty nat'ral, don't she, Bill? Remember when we trucked her up from the freight station and dumped her in three year ago? She was the *Nymph* then. Gol, how happy that kid was—you remember, Bill? I'll tell *you* kids now what I told him then—told him right in front of his father; I says, 'Harry, you remember she's human and treat her as such,' that's what I says ter him. *You* remember, Bill."

Roy noticed that the girl had strolled away and was standing in the gathering darkness a few yards distant, gazing at the boat. The clumsy looking hull, in which the boys had taken refuge, seemed trim and graceful now, and Roy was reminded of the fairy story of the ugly duckling, who was really a swan, but whose wondrous beauty was unappreciated until it found itself among its own kindred.

"Yes, sir, that's wot I told him, 'cause I've lived on the river here all my life, ain't I, Bill, an' I know. Yer don't give an automobile no name, an' yer don't give an airyplane no name, an' yer don't give a motorcycle nor a bicycle no name, but yer give a boat a name 'cause she's human. She'll be cranky and stubborn an' then she'll be soft and amiable as pie—that's 'cause she's human. An' that's why a man'll let a old boat stan' an' rot ruther'n sell it. 'Cause it's human and it kinder gets him. You treat her as such, you boys."

"How did Harry Stanton die?" Tom asked.

The man, with a significant motion of his finger toward the lone figure of the girl, drew nearer and the boys gathered about him.

"The old gent didn' tell ye, hey?"

"Not a word."

"Hmmm—well, Harry was summat older'n you boys, he was gettin' to be a reg'lar young man. Trouble with him was he didn' know what he wanted. First off, he must have a horse, 'n' then he must have a boat, so th' old man, he got him this boat. He's crusty, but he's all to the good, th' old man is."

"You bet your life he is," said Pee-wee.

"Well, Harry an' Benty Willis—you remember Benty, Bill—him an' Benty Willis was out in the *Nymph*—that's this here very boat. They had 'er anchored up a ways here, right off Cerry's Hill, an' they was out in the skiff floppin' 'round—some said fishin'."

"They was bobbin' fer eels, that's wot they was doin'," said the other man.

"Well, wotever they was doin' it was night 'n' thar was a storm. An' that's every bloomin' thing me or you or anybody else'll ever know about it. The next day Croby Risbeck up here was out fer his nets an' he come on the skiff swamped, over there off'n that point. An' near it was Benty Willis."

"Drowned?" asked Roy.

"Drownded. He must o' tried to keep afloat by clingin' t' the skiff, but she was down to her gunnel an' wouldn' keep a cat afloat. He might o' kep' his head out o' water a spell clingin' to it. All I know is he was drownded when he was found. Wotever become o' that skiff, Bill?"

"And what about Mr. Stanton's son?" Roy asked.

"Well, they got his hat an' his coat that he must a' thrown off an' that's all. Th' old man 'ud never look at the launch again. He had her brought over'n' tied up right about here, an' there she stood till the floods carried her up over this here road and sot her down in the marsh."

"Did the skiff belong with her?" Roy asked.

"Sure enough; always taggin' on behind."

Percy K. Fitzhugh

"How did they think it happened?" asked Tom.

"Wall, fer one thing, it was a rough night an' they may uv jest got swamped. But agin, it's a fact that Harry knew how to swim; he was a reg'lar water-rat. Now, what I think is this. Th' only thing 't 'd prevent that lad gettin' ashore'd be his gettin' killed—not drowned, but *killed*."

"You don't mean murdered?" Tom asked.

"Well, if they was swamped by the big night boat, an' he got mixed up with the paddle wheel, I don't know if ye'd call it murder, but it'd be killin', sure enough. Leastways, they never got him, an' it's my belief he was chopped up. Take a tip from me, you boys, an' look out fer the night boat, 'cause the night boat ain't a-goin' t' look out fer you."

The girl, strolling back, put an end to their talk, but it was clear that she, too, must have been thinking of that fatal night, for her eyes were red and she seemed less vivacious.

"You must be careful," said she, "there are a good many accidents on the river. My father told me to tell you you'd better not do much traveling at night. I want to see you on board, and then I must go home," she added.

She held out her hand and Roy, who was in this instance best suited to speak for the three, grasped it.

"There's no use trying to thank you and your father," he said. "If you'd given us some little thing we could thank you, but it seems silly to say just the same thing when we have a thing like this given to us, and yet it seems worse for us to go away without saying anything. I guess you know what I mean."

"You must promise to be careful—can you all swim?"

"We are scouts," laughed Roy.

"And that means you can do anything, I suppose."

"No, not that," Roy answered, "but we do want to tell you how much we thank you—you and your father."

"Especially you," put in Pee-wee.

She smiled, a pretty wistful smile, and her eyes glistened. "You did more for me," she said, "you got my bird back. I care more for that bird than I could ever care for any boat. My brother brought it to me from Costa Rica."

She stepped back to the auto. The chauffeur was already in his place, and the two men were coiling up their ropes and piling the heavy planks and rollers on board the truck. The freshly painted boat was growing dim in the gathering darkness and the lordly hills across the river were paling into gray again. As the little group paused, a deep, melodious whistle re-echoed from the towering heights and the great night boat came into view, her lights aloft, plowing up midstream. The *Good Turn* bobbed humbly like a good subject as the mighty white giant passed. The girl watched the big steamer wistfully and for a moment no one spoke.

"Was your brother—fond of traveling?" Roy ventured.

"Yes, he was crazy for it," she answered, "and you can't bring *him* back as you brought my bird back—you *can't* do everything after all."

It was Tom Slade who spoke now. "We couldn't do any more than try," said he. He spoke in that dull, heavy manner, and it annoyed Roy, for it seemed as if he were making fun of the girl's bereavement.

Percy K. Fitzhugh

Perhaps it seemed the same to her, for she turned the subject at once. "I'm going to sit here until you are in the boat," she said.

They pulled the *Good Turn* as near the shore as they could bring her without grounding for the tide was running out, and Pee-wee held her with the rope while the others went aboard over a plank laid from the shore to the deck. Then Pee-wee followed, hurrying, for there was nothing to hold her now.

They clambered up on the cabin, Roy waving the naval flag, and Pee-wee the name pennant, while Tom cast the anchor, for already the *Good Turn* was drifting.

"Good-bye!" they cried.

"Good-bye!" she called back, waving her handkerchief as the auto started, "and good luck to you!"

"We'll try to do a good turn some day to make up," shouted Pee-wee.

CHAPTER IX

THE MYSTERY

"What I don't understand," said Tom, in his dull way, "is how if that fellow was drowned or killed that night, he managed to get back to this boat again—that's what gets me."

"What?" said Roy.

"What are you talking about?" chimed in Pee-wee.

They were sitting in the little cabin of the *Good Turn* eating rice cakes, about an hour after the launching. The boat rocked gently at its moorings, the stars glittered in the wide expanse of water, the tiny lights in the neighboring village kept them cheery company as they chatted there in the lonesome night with the hills frowning down upon them. It was very quiet and this, no less than the joyous sense of possession of this cosy home, kept them up, notwithstanding their strenuous two days of labor.

"Just what I said," said Tom. "See that board you fixed the oil stove on? I believe that was part of that skiff. You can see the letters N-Y-M-P-H even under the paint. That strip was in the boat all the time. How did it get here? That's what *I'd*

Percy K. Fitzhugh

like to know."

Roy laid down his "flopper" and examined the board carefully, the excited Pee-wee joining him. It was evidently the upper strip of the side planking from a rowboat and at one end, under the diluted paint which they had here used, could be dimly traced the former name of the launch.

"What-do-you-know-about-that?" ejaculated Roy.

"It's a regular mystery," said Pee-wee; "that's one thing I like, a mystery."

"If that's a part of this boat's skiff," said Tom, "then it proves two things. It proves that the boat was damaged—no fellow could pull a plank from it like that; and it proves that that fellow came back to the launch. It proves that he was injured, too. That man said he could swim. Then why should he bring this board back with him unless it was to help him keep afloat?"

"He wouldn't need to drag it aboard," said Roy.

"Now you spoil it all," put in Pee-wee.

"I don't know anything about that," said Tom, "but that board didn't drift back and climb in by itself. It must have been here all the time. I suppose the other fellow—the one they found drowned—*might* have got it here, some way," he added.

"Not likely," said Roy. "If he'd managed to get back to the launch with the board, he wouldn't have jumped overboard again just to get drowned. He'd have managed to stay aboard."

There was silence for a few minutes while Roy drummed on the plank with his fingers and Pee-wee could hardly repress his excitement at the thought that they were on the track of a real adventure. Tom Slade had "gone and done it again." He was always surprising them by his stolid announcement of some discovery which opened up delectable possibilities. And smile as he would (especially in view of Pee-wee's exuberance), Roy could not but see that here was something of very grave significance.

"That's what I meant," drawled Tom, "when I told her that we could *try*—to find her brother."

This was a knockout blow.

"This trip of ours is going to be just like a book," prophesied Pee-wee, excitedly; "there's a—there's a—long lost brother, and—and—a deep mystery!"

"Sure," said Roy. "We'll have to change our names; I'll be Roy Rescue, you be Pee-wee Pinkerton, the boy sleuth, and Tom'll be Tom Trustful. What d'you say, Tom?"

Tom made no answer and for all Roy's joking, he was deeply interested. Like most important clues, the discovery was but a little thing, yet it could not be accounted for except on the theory that Harry Stanton had somehow gotten back to the launch after the accident, whatever the accident was. It meant just that—nothing less and nothing more; though, indeed, it did mean more to Pee-wee and as he slept that night, in the gently rocking boat, he dreamed that he had vowed a solemn vow to Mr. Stanton's daughter to "find her brother or perish in the attempt." He carried a brace of pistols, and sailing forth with his trusty chums, he landed in the island of Madagascar, to which Harry Stanton had been carried, bound hand and foot, in an aeroplane. The three,

Percy K. Fitzhugh

undaunted, then built a Zeppelin and sailed up to the summit of a dizzy crag where they rescued the kidnapped youth and on reaching home, Mr. Stanton gave them a sea-going yacht and a million dollars each for pocket money. When he awoke from this thrilling experience he found that the *Good Turn* was chugging leisurely up the river in the broad daylight.

The boat behaved very well, indeed. She leaked a little from the strain of launching, but the engine pumped the water out faster than it came in. All day long they lolled in the cockpit or on the cabin roof, taking turns at the steering. Roy, who best understood gas engines, attended to the motor, but it needed very little attention except that it missed on high speed, so he humored it and they ambled along at "sumpty-sump miles an hour," as Roy said, "but what care we," he added, "as long as she goes." They anchored for several hours in the middle of the day and fished, and had a mess of fresh perch for luncheon.

Naturally, the topic of chief interest was the possibility that Harry Stanton was living, but the clue which appeared to indicate that much suggested nothing further, and the question of why he did not return home, if he were indeed alive was a puzzling one.

"His sister said he had been to Costa Rica, and was fond of traveling," suggested Tom. "Maybe his parents objected to his going away from home so he went this way—as long as the chance came to him—and let them think he was drowned."

Roy, sitting on the cabin roof with his knees drawn up, shook his head. "Or maybe he left the boat again and tried to swim to shore to go home, and didn't make it," he added.

"That's possible," said Tom, "but then they'd probably have

found his body."

"We aren't sure he's alive," Roy said thoughtfully, "but it means a whole lot not to be sure that he's dead."

"Maybe he was made away with by someone who wanted the boat," said Pee-wee. "Maybe a convict from the prison killed him—you never can tell. Jiminys, it's a mystery, sure."

"You bet it is," said Roy. "The plot grows thicker. If Sir Guy Weatherby were only here, or Detective Darewell—or some of those story-book ginks they—"

"They probably wouldn't have noticed the plank from the skiff," suggested Pee-wee.

Roy laughed and then fell to thinking. "Gee, it would be great if we could find him!" he said.

And there the puzzling matter ended, for the time being; but the *Good Turn* took on a new interest because of the mystery with which it was associated and Pee-wee was continually edifying his companions with startling and often grewsome theories as to the fate or present whereabouts of Harry Stanton, until—until that thing happened which turned all their thoughts from this puzzle and proved that bad turns as well as good ones have the boomerang quality of returning upon their author.

It was the third afternoon of their cruise, or their "flop" as Roy called it, for they had flopped along rather than cruised, and the *Good Turn's* course would have indicated, as he remarked, a fit of the blind staggers. They had paused to fish and to bathe; they had thrown together a makeshift aquaplane from the pieces of an old float which they had found, and had ridden gayly upon it; and their course had been so leisurely and rambling that they had not yet reached Poughkeepsie, when all of a sudden the engine stopped.

Roy went through the usual course of procedure to start it up, but without result. There was not a kick left in it. Silently he unscrewed the cap on the deck, pushed a stick into the tank and lifted it out—dry.

"Boys," said he, solemnly, "there is not a drop of gasoline in the tank. The engine must have used it all up. Probably it has been using it all the time—"

"You make me sick," said Pee-wee.

"I have known engines to do that before."

"Didn't I tell you to get gasoline in Newburgh?" demanded Pee-wee.

"You did, Sir Walter, and would that we had taken your advice; but I trusted the engine and it has evidently been using the gasoline while our backs were turned. *We* should worry! You don't suppose it would run on witch hazel, do you?"

"Didn't I tell—" began Pee-wee.

"If we could only reduce friend Walter to a liquid," said Roy. "I think we could get started all right—he's so explosive."

"Bright boy," said Tom.

"Oh, I'm a regular feller, I am," said Roy. "I knew that engine would stop when there wasn't any more gasoline—I just felt it in my bones. But what care we!

'Oh, we are merry mountaineers,
And have no carking cares or fears—
Or gasoline.'

Get out the oars, scouts!"

So they got out the oars and with the aid of these and a paddle succeeded in making the shore where they tied up to the dilapidated remnants of what had once been a float.

"There must be a village in the neighborhood," said Tom, "or there wouldn't be a float here."

"Sherlock Holmes Slade is at it again," said Roy. It would have been a pretty serious accident that Roy wouldn't have taken gayly. "Pee-wee, you're appointed a committee to look after the boat while Tomasso and I go in search of adventure —and gasoline. There must be a road up there somewhere and if there's a road I dare say we can find a garage—maybe even a village. Get things ready for supper, Pee-wee, and when we get back I'll make a Silver Fox omelet for good luck."

The spot where they had made a landing was at the foot of precipitous hills between which and the shore ran the railroad tracks. Tom and Roy, carrying a couple of gasoline cans, started along a road which led around the lower reaches of one of these hills. As Pee-wee stood upon the cabin watching them, the swinging cans were brightened by the rays of the declining sun, and there was a chill in the air as the familiar grayness fell upon the heights, bringing to the boy that sense of loneliness which he had felt before.

He was of the merriest temperament, was Pee-wee, and, as he had often said, not averse to "being jollied." But he was withal very sensitive and during the trip he had more than once fancied that Tom and Roy had fallen together to his own exclusion, and it awakened in him now and then a feeling that he was the odd number of the party. He had tried to ingratiate himself with them, though to be sure no particular effort was needed to do that, yet sometimes he saw, or fancied he saw, little things which made him feel that in important matters he was left out of account. Roy would slap him on the shoulder and tousle his hair, but he would ask Tom's advice—and take it. Perhaps Roy had allowed his propensity for banter and jollying to run too far in his treatment of Pee-wee. At all events, the younger boy had found himself a bit chagrined at times that their discussions had not been wholly three-handed. And now, as he watched the others hiking off through the twilight, and heard their laughter, he recalled that it was usually *he* who was appointed a "committee to stay and watch the boat."

This is not a pleasant train of thought when you are standing alone in the bleakness and sadness and growing chill of the dying day, with tremendous nature piled all about you, and watching your two companions as they disappear along a lonely road. But the mood was upon him and it did not cheer him when Roy, turning and making a megaphone of his hands, called, "Look out and don't fall into the gas tank, Pee-wee!"

He *had* reminded them that they had better buy gasoline at Newburgh, while they had the chance. Roy had answered jokingly telling Pee-wee that he had better buy a soda in the city while *he* had the chance, and Tom had added, "I guess the kid thinks we want to drink it."

Well, there they were hiking it up over the hills now in quest of gasoline and still joking him.

If Pee-wee had remembered Roy's generous pleasure in the

"parrot stunt," he would have been much happier, but instead he allowed his imagination to picture Tom and Roy in the neighboring village, having a couple of sodas—perhaps taking a flyer at a movie show.

He did as much as he could toward getting supper, and when it grew dark and still they did not return, he clambered up on the cabin roof again and sat there gazing off into the night. But still they did not come.

"Gee, I'm a Silver Fox, anyway," he said; "you'd think he'd want one of his own patrol with him *sometimes*—gee!"

He rose and went down into the cabin where the dollar watch which hung on a nail told him that it was eight o'clock. Then it occurred to him that it would serve them right if he got his own supper and was in his bunk and asleep when they returned. It would be a sort of revenge on them. He would show them, at least, that he could get along very well by himself, and by way of doing so he would make some rice cakes. Roy was not the only one who could make rice cakes. He, Pee-wee, could make them if nobody stood by guying him.

He had never wielded the flopper; that had been Roy's province; but he could, all right, he told himself. So he dug into Roy's duffel bag for the recipe book which was famous in the troop; which told the secrets of the hunter's stew; which revealed the mystery of plum-duff and raisin pop-overs in all their luscious details and which set you on the right path for the renowned rice cakes.

Between the leaves, right where the rice cake recipe revealed itself to the hungry inquirer, was a folded paper which dropped out as Pee-wee opened the book. For all he knew it contained the recipe so he held it under the lantern and read:

"Dear Mary:

"Since you butted in, Tom and I have decided that it would be better for Pee-wee to go with *him*, and I'll stay home. Anyway, that's what I've decided. So you'll get your wish all right and I should worry.

"Roy."

Pee-wee read it twice over, then he laid it on the locker and sat down and looked at it. Then he picked it up and read it over again. He did not even realize that its discovery among Roy's things would indicate that it had never been sent. Sent or not, it had been written.

So this was the explanation of Roy's invitation that he accompany them on the trip. Mary Temple had asked them to let him go. Yet, despite his present mood, he could not believe that his own patrol leader, Roy Blakeley, could have written this.

"I bet Tom Slade is—I bet he's the cause of it," he said.

He recalled now how he had talked about the trip to Mary Temple and how she had spoken rather mysteriously about the possibility of his going along. So it was she who was his good friend; it was to her he owed the invitation which had come to him with such a fine air of sincerity.

"I always—crinkums, anyway girls always seem to like me, that's one thing," he said. "And—and Roy did, too, before Tom Slade came into the troop."

It was odd how he turned against Tom, making him the scapegoat for Roy's apparent selfishness and hypocrisy.

"They just brought me along for charity, like," he said, "'cause she told them to. Cracky, anyway, I didn't try to make her do that—I didn't."

This revelation in black and white of Roy's real feeling overcame him and as he put the letter back in the book and the book back in the duffel bag, he could scarcely keep his hand from trembling.

"Anyway, I knew it all the time," he said. "I could see it."

He had no appetite for rice cakes now. He took some cakes of chocolate and a couple of hard biscuits and stuffed them in his pocket. Then he went out into the cockpit and listened. There was no sound of voices or footfalls, nothing but the myriad voices of nature, or frogs croaking nearby, of a cheery cricket somewhere on shore, of the water lapping against the broken old wharf as the wind drove it in shoreward.

He returned to the cabin, tore a leaf from his scout notebook and wrote, but he had to blink his eyes to keep back the tears.

"Dear Roy:

"I think you'll have more fun if you two go the rest of the way alone. I always said two's a company, three's a crowd. You've heard me say it and I ought to have had sense enough to remember it. But anyway, I'm not mad and I like you just as much. I'll see you at camp.

"WALTER HARRIS."

"P. S.—If I had to vote again for patrol leader I'd vote for you."

Percy K. Fitzhugh

He was particular not to mention Tom by name and to address his note to Roy. He laid it in the frying pan on the stove (in which he had intended to make the rice cakes) and then, with his duffel bag over his shoulder and his scout staff in hand, he stepped from the *Good Turn*, listening cautiously for approaching footsteps, and finding the way clear he stole away through the darkness.

CHAPTER X

PEE-WEE'S ADVENTURE

A walk of a few yards or so brought him to the railroad track. He was no longer the clown and mascot of the *Good Turn*; he was the scout, alert, resourceful, bent on hiding his tracks.

He did not know where he was going, more than that he was going to elude pursuit and find a suitable spot in which to camp for the night. Matters would take care of themselves in the daytime. He wanted to follow the railroad tracks, for he knew that would keep him close to the river, but he knew also that it had the disadvantage of being the very thing the boys would suppose it most likely that he would do. For, feel as he would toward them, he did not for a moment believe that they would let him take himself off without searching for him. And he knew something of Tom Slade's ability as a tracker.

"They won't get any merit badges trailing *me*, though," he said.

So he crossed the tracks and walked a couple of hundred feet or so up a hill, grabbed the limb of a tree, swung up into its branches, let himself down on the other side, and retraced his steps to the tracks and began to walk the ties, northward. He was now thoroughly in the spirit of the escapade and a feeling of independence seized him, a feeling that every scout knows, that having undertaken a thing he must succeed in it.

A walk of about ten minutes brought him to a high, roofed platform beside the tracks, where one or two hogsheads were standing and several cases. But there was no sign of life or habitation. It was evidently the freight station for some town not far distant, for a couple of old-fashioned box-cars stood on a siding, and Pee-wee contemplated them with the joy of sudden inspiration.

"Crinkums, that would be a dandy place to sleep," he thought, for it was blowing up cold and he had but scant equipment.

He went up to the nearest car and felt of the sliding door. It was the least bit open, owing to its damaged condition, and by moving it a very few inches more he could have slipped inside. But he paused to examine the pasters and chalk marks on the body. One read "Buffalo—4—LLM." There were the names of various cities and numerous strange marks. It was evident the car had been quite a globe-trotter in its time, but as it stood there then it seemed to Pee-wee that so it must have stood for a dozen years and was likely to stand for a dozen years more.

He slid the door a little farther open on its rusty hinges and climbed inside. It was very dark and still and smelled like a stable, but suddenly he was aware of a movement not far from him. He did not exactly hear it, but he felt that something was moving. For a moment a cold shudder went over him and he stood stark still, not daring to move. Then, believing that his imagination had played a trick, he fumbled in his duffel bag, found his flashlight and sent its vivid gleam about the car. A young fellow in a convict's suit stood menacingly before the door with one hand upon it, blinking and watching the boy with a lowering aspect. His head was close-shaven and shone in the light's glare so that he looked hardly human. He had apparently sprung to the door, perhaps out of a sound sleep, and he was evidently greatly alarmed. Pee-wee was also greatly alarmed, but he was no coward and he stood his ground though his heart was pounding in his breast.

"You ain't no bo," said the man.

"I—I'm a scout," stammered Pee-wee, "and I was going to camp here for the night. I didn't know there was anyone here."

The man continued to glare at him and Pee-wee thought he had never in his life seen such a villainous face.

"I'll—I'll go away," he said, "I was only going to sleep here."

The convict, still guarding the door, leered brutally at him, his head hanging low, his lips apart, more like a beast than a man.

"No, yer won't go 'way, nuther," he finally said; "yer ain't goin' ter double-cross *me*, pal. Wot d'yer say yer wuz?"

"A scout," said Pee-wee. "I don't need to stay here, you were here first. I can camp outdoors."

"No, yer don't," said the man. "You stay whar yer are. Yer ain't goin' ter double-cross *me*."

"I don't know what you mean by that," said Pee-wee.

Percy K. Fitzhugh

The convict did not offer him any explanation, only stood guarding the door with a threatening aspect, which very much disconcerted Pee-wee. He was a scout and he was brave, and not panicky in peril or emergency, but the striped clothing and cropped head and stupid leer of the man before him made him seem something less than human. His terror was more that of an animal than of a man and his apparent inability to express himself save by the repetition of that one sentence frightened the boy. Apparently the creature was all instinct and no brains.

"Yer gotta stay here," he repeated. "Yer ain't goin' ter double-cross *me*, pal."

Then it began to dawn on Pee-wee what he meant.

"I guess I know about you," he said, "because I heard about your—getting away. But, anyway, if you let me go away I won't tell anyone I saw you. I don't want to camp here now. I'll promise not to go and tell people, if that's what you're afraid of."

"Wot's in that bag?" asked the man.

"My camping things."

"Got any grub?"

"I've got two biscuits and some chocolate."

"Gimme it," said the man, coming closer.

He snatched the food as fast as it was taken out of the bag, and Pee-wee surmised that he had not eaten since his escape from prison for he devoured it ravenously like a famished beast.

"Got any more?" he asked, glaring into the boy's face menacingly.

"No, I'm sorry I haven't. I escaped, too, as you might say, from my friends—from the fellers I was with. And I only brought a little with me."

After a few minutes (doubtless from the stimulating effects of the food), the convict's fear seemed to subside somewhat and he spoke a little more freely. But Pee-wee found it very unpleasant being shut in with him there in the darkness, for, of course, the flashlight could not be kept burning all the time.

"I wouldn't do yer no hurt," he assured Pee-wee. "I t'ought mebbe yer wuz a *de*-coy. Yer ain't, are ye?" he asked suspiciously.

"No, I'm not," said Pee-wee, "I'm just what I told you—"

"I ain't goin' ter leave ye go free, so ye might's well shut up. I seen pals double-cross *me*—them ez I trusted, too. Yer square, I guess—only innercent."

"I'd keep my word even with—I'd keep my word with you," said Pee-wee, "just the same as with anyone. Besides, I don't see what's the use of keeping me here. You'll have to let me go some time, you can't keep me here forever, and you can't stay here forever, yourself."

"If ye stan' right 'n' show ye're game," said the convict, "thar won't no hurt come to ye. This here car's way-billed fer Buff'lo, 'n' I'm waitin' ter be took up now. It's a grain car. Yer ain't goin' ter peach wot I tell ye, now? I wuz put wise to it afore I come out by a railroad bloke. I had it straight these here cars would be picked up fer Buff'lo the nex' day after I done my trick. But they ain't took 'em up yet, an' I'm close ter starvin' here."

Pee-wee could not help but feel a certain sympathy with this man, wretch though he was, who on the information of some accomplice outside the prison, had made his escape expecting to be carried safely away the next day and had been crouching, half-starved, in this freight car ever since, waiting.

"What will you do if they don't take up the car for a week?" he asked. "They might look inside of it, too; or they might change their minds about taking it."

He was anxious for himself for he contemplated with terror his threatened imprisonment, but he could not help being concerned also for this miserable creature and he wondered what would happen if they both remained in the car for several days more, with nothing to eat. Then, surely, the man would be compelled to put a little faith in him and let him go out in search of food. He wondered what he should do in that case—what he ought to do; but that, he realized, was borrowing trouble. Mr. Ellsworth, his scoutmaster, had once said that it is *always bad to play false*. Well, then, would it be bad to play false with an escaped felon—to double-cross him? Pee-wee did not know.

His companion interrupted his train of thought "They don' look inside o' way-billed empties—not much," he said, "an' they don't let 'em stan' so long, nuther. I got bad luck, I did, from doin' my trick on a Friday. They'll be 'long pretty quick, though. They reckisitioned all th' empty grain cars fer Buff'lo. I'm lookin' ter hear th' whistle any minute, I am, an' I got a pal waitin' fer me in the yards up ter Buff'lo, wid the duds. When I get there 'n' get me clo's changed, mebbe I'll leave ye come back if me pal 'n' me thinks ye kin be trusted."

"I can be trusted now just as much as I could be trusted then," said Pee-wee, greatly disturbed at the thought of this enforced journey; "and how could I get back? I guess maybe you don't know anything about scouts—maybe they weren't started when you were—Anyway, a scout can be trusted. Anybody'll tell you that. If he gives his word he'll keep it. I don't know anything about what you did and if you ask me if I want to see you get captured I couldn't tell you, because I don't know how I feel. But if you'll let me go now I'll promise not to say anything to anyone. I don't want to go to Buffalo. I want to go to my camp. As long as I know about you, you got to trust me some time and you might as well trust me now."

If the fugitive could have seen Pee-wee's earnest face and honest eyes as he made this pitiful appeal, he might have softened a little, even if he had not appreciated the good sense of the boy's remarks.

"I'd ruther get me other duds on fust, 'n' I'd like fer ter hev ye meet me pal," he said, with the first touch of humor he had shown. "Now, if yer go ter cuttin' up a rumpus I'll jest hev ter brain ye, see?"

Pee-wee leaned back against the side of the car in the darkness as despair seized him. He had always coveted adventure but this was too much and he felt himself to be utterly helpless in this dreadful predicament. Even as he stood there in a state of pitiable consternation, a shrill whistle sounded in the distance, which was echoed back from the unseen hills.

"Dat's a freight," said the convict, quickly.

Pee-wee listened and his last flickering hope was exting-uished as he recognized the discordant rattle and bang of the slow-moving train, emphasized by the stillness of the night. Nearer and nearer it came and louder grew the clank and clamor of the miscellaneous procession of box cars. It was a freight, all right.

"If—if you'll let me get out," Pee-wee began, on the very verge of a panic, "if you'll let me get out—"

The convict fumblingly took him by the throat. He could feel the big, coarse, warm fingers pressing into the sides of his neck and it gagged him.

"If yer open yer head when we're bein' took up, I'll brain yer, hear that?" he said. "Gimme that light, gimme yer knife."

He flashed on the light, tore the scout knife from Pee-wee's belt, and flung the frightened boy against the side of the car. Keeping the light pointed at him, he opened the knife. The spirit of desperate resolve seemed to have reawakened within him at the sound of that long-hoped-for train and Pee-wee was no more to him than an insect to have his life trampled out if he could not be used or if his use were unavailing. Here, unmasked, was the man who had braved the tempestuous river on that dreadful night. Truly, as the sheriff had said, "desperate characters will take desperate chances."

"If yer open yer head or call out or make a noise wid yer feet or poun' de side o' de car or start a-bawlin' I'll brain ye, ye hear? Nobody gets *me* alive. An' if anybody comes in here 'cause o' you makin' a noise and cryin' fer help, yer'll be the fust to git croaked—see?"

He pointed the light straight at Pee-wee, holding the open jack-knife in his other hand, and glared at him with a look which struck terror to the boy's heart. Pee-wee was too frightened and exhausted to answer. He only shook his head in acknowledgment, breathing heavily.

In a few minutes the train had come abreast of them and stopped. They could hear the weary puffing of the engine, and voices calling and occasionally they caught the gleam of a lantern through the crack in the car. Pee-wee remained very still. The convict took his stand in the middle of the car between the two sliding doors, lowering and alert, holding the flashlight and the clasp knife.

Soon the train moved again, then stopped. There were calls from one end of it to the other. Then it started again and continued to move until Pee-wee thought it was going away, and his hope revived at the thought that escape might yet be possible. Then the sound came nearer again and presently the car received a jolt, accompanied by a bang. The convict was thrown a little, but he resumed his stand, waiting, desperate, menacing. Those few minutes must have been dreadful ones to him as he watched the two doors, knife in hand.

Then came more shunting and banging and calling and answering, a short, shrill whistle and more moving and then at last the slow, continuous progress of the car, which was evidently now at last a part of that endless miscellaneous procession, rattling along through the night with its innumerable companions.

"It's lucky for them," said the convict, through his teeth, as he relaxed.

Pee-wee hardly knew what he meant, he had scarcely any interest, and it was difficult to hear on account of the noise. He was too shaken up to think clearly, but he wondered, as the rattling train moved slowly along, how long he could go without food, how he would get back from Buffalo, and whether this dreadful companion of his would take his stand, like an animal at bay, whenever the train stopped.

After a little time, when he was able to get a better grip on himself and realize fully his terrible plight, he began to think how, after all, the scout, with all his resource and fine courage, his tracking and his trailing and his good turns, is pretty helpless in a real dilemma. Here was an adventure, and rather too much of a one, and neither he nor any other scout could extricate him from his predicament. In books they could have done it with much brave talk, but in real life they could do nothing. He was tired and frightened and helpless; the shock of the pressure of those brutal fingers about his neck still distressed him, and his head ached from it all.

What wonder if in face of this tragical reality, the scouts with all their much advertised resource and prowess should lose prestige a little in his thoughts? Yet it might have been worth while for him to pause and reflect that though the scout arm is neither brutal nor menacing, it still has an exceedingly long reach and that it can pin you just as surely as the cruel fingers which had fixed themselves on his own throat.

But he was too terrified and exhausted to think very clearly about anything.

CHAPTER XI

TRACKS AND TRAILING

When the engineer blew the whistle which the convict had heard with such satisfaction and Pee-wee with such dread, it was by way of warning two dark figures which were about to cross the tracks. Something bright which they carried shone in the glare of the headlight.

"Here comes a freight," said Tom.

"Let it come, I can't stop it," said Roy. "Je-ru-salem, this can is heavy."

"Same here," said Tom.

"I wouldn't carry another can of gas this far for a prince's ransom—whatever in the dickens that is. Look at the blisters on my hand, will you? Gee, I'm so hungry I could eat a package of tacks. I bet Pee-wee's been throwing duck fits. Never mind, we did a good turn. 'We seen our duty and we done it noble.' Some grammar! They ought to put us on the cover of the manual. Boy scouts returning from a gasoline hunt! Good turn, turn down the gas, hey? Did you ever try tracking a freight train? It's terribly exciting."

"Keep still, will you!" said Tom, setting down his can. "Can't you see I'm spilling the gasoline? Don't make me laugh."

"The face with the smile wins," Roy rattled on. "For he ain't no slouch, but the lad with the grouch—Pick up your can and get off the track—safety first!"

"Well, then, for goodness' sake, shut up!" laughed Tom.

It had been like this all the way back, Tom setting down his can at intervals and laughing in spite of himself at Roy's nonsense.

When they reached the boat Roy looked inside and called Pee-wee.

"Where is our young hero, anyway?" he said.

But "our young hero" was not there. They poured the gas into the tank and then went inside where Roy discovered the note in the saucepan. He read it, then handed it to Tom and the two stood for a moment staring at each other, too surprised to speak.

"What do you suppose has got into him?" exclaimed Tom.

"Search me; unless he's mad because we left him here."

Tom looked about as if in search of some explanation, and as usual his scrutiny was not unfruitful.

"It looks as if he had started to get supper," said he: "there's the rice—"

A sudden inspiration seized Roy. Pulling out the recipe book from his duffel bag he opened it where the letter to Mary

Temple lay. "I thought so," he said shamefacedly. "I left the end of it sticking out to mark the place and now it's in between the leaves. That's what did the mischief; he must have found it."

"You ought to have torn it up before we started," said Tom.

"I know it, but I just stuck it in there when I was brushing up my memory on rice cakes, and there it's been ever since. I ought never to have written it at all, if it comes to that."

Tom made no answer. They had never mentioned that incident which was such an unpleasant memory to them both.

"Well, we've got to find him, that's all," said Tom.

"Gee, it seems as if we couldn't possibly get along without Pee-wee now," Roy said. "I never realized how much fun it would be having him along. Poor kid! It serves me right for—"

"What's the use of thinking about that *now*?" said Tom, bluntly. "We've just got to find him Come on, hurry up, get your flashlight. Every minute we wait he's a couple of hund-red feet farther away."

For the first time in all their trip, as it seemed to Roy, Tom's spirit and interest were fully aroused. He was as keen as a bloodhound for the trail and instinctively Roy obeyed him.

They hurried out without waiting for so much as a bite to eat and with the aid of their flashlights (and thanks to the recent rains) had no difficulty in trailing Pee-wee as far as the railroad tracks.

"He'd either follow the track," said Tom, "or else the road we took and hide somewhere till we passed. He wouldn't try any cross-country business at night, I don't believe."

"Poor kid!" was all Roy could say. The thought of that note which he had carelessly left about and of Pee-wee starting out alone haunted him and made him feel like a scoundrel. All his gayety had vanished and he depended on Tom and followed his lead. He remembered only too well the wonderful tracking stunt that Tom had done the previous summer, and now, as he looked at that rather awkward figure, kneeling with head low, and creeping along from tie to tie, oblivious to all but his one purpose, he felt a certain thrill of confidence. By a sort of unspoken understanding, he (who was the most all-round scout of them all and looked it into the bargain) had acted as their leader and spokesman on the trip; and Tom Slade, who could no more talk to strangers, and especially girls, than he could fly, had followed, envying Roy's easy manner and all-around proficiency. But Tom was a wizard in tracking, and as Roy watched him now he could not help realizing with a pang of shame that again it was Tom who had come to the rescue to save him from the results of his own selfishness and ill-temper. He remembered those words, spoken in Tom's stolid way on the night of their quarrel. "*It's kind of like a trail in your mind and I got to hit the right trail.*" He *had* hit the right trail then and brought Roy to his senses, and now again when that rude, selfish note cropped up to work mischief it was Tom who knelt down there on the railroad tracks, seeking again for the right trail.

"Here it is," he said at last, when he had closely examined and smelt of a dark spot on one of the ties. "Lucky you let him clean the engine; he must have been standing in the oil trough."

"Good he had his sneaks on, too," said Roy, stooping. "It's

like a stamp on a pound of butter."

It was not quite as clear as that, but if Pee-wee had prepared his sneaks especially for making prints on wooden ties he could scarcely have done better. In order to get at the main bearings of the engine he had, with characteristic disregard, stood plunk in the copper drain basin under the crank-case. The oil had undoubtedly softened the rubber sole of his sneakers so that it held the clinging substance, and in some cases it was possible to distinguish on the ties the half-obliterated crisscross design of the rubber sole.

"Come on," said Tom, "this thing is a cinch."

"It's a shame to call it tracking," said Roy, regaining some measure of his wonted spirits as they hurried along. "It's a blazed trail."

And so, indeed, it was while it lasted, but suddenly it ceased and the boys paused, puzzled.

"Listen for trains," warned Tom.

"There won't be any along yet a while," said Roy. "There's one stopped up there a ways now."

They could hear the shunting up the track, interspersed with faint voices calling.

"Here's where he's put one over on us," said Roy. "Poor kid."

"Here's where he's been reading Sir Baden-Powell, you mean. Wait till I see if he worked the boomerang trick. See that tree up there?"

It was amazing how readily Tom assumed that Pee-wee

would do just what he had done to elude pursuit.

"Tree's always a suspicious thing," said he; "this is a Boer wrinkle—comes from South Africa."

He did not bother hunting for the tracks in the hubbly ground, but made straight for the tree.

"Poor kid," was all he could say as he picked up a few freshly fallen leaves and a twig or two. "He's good at climbing anyway." He examined one of the leaves carefully with his flashlight. "Squint around," he said to Roy, "and see if you can find where he stuck his staff in the ground."

Roy got down, poking his light here and there, and parting the rough growth.

"Here it is," said he.

Oh, it was all easy—too easy, for a scout. It gave them no feeling of triumph, only pity for the stout-hearted little fellow who had tried to escape them.

A more careful examination of the lower branches of the tree and of the ground beneath was enough. Tom did not even bother about the prints leading back to the railroad, but went back to the tracks and after a few minutes picked up the trail again there. This they followed till they came to the siding, now deserted.

Here, for a few minutes, it did seem as if Pee-wee had succeeded in baffling them, for the prints leaving the ties ran over to the siding and there ended in a confused collection of footprints pointing in every direction. Evidently, Pee-wee had paused here, but what direction he had taken from this point they could not see.

"This has got *me* guessing," said Tom.

"He was tangoing around here," said Roy, pointing his flashlight to the ground, "that's sure. Maybe the little Indian walked the rail."

But an inspection of the rail showed that he had not done that, unless, indeed, the recent rain had obliterated the marks.

They examined the platform carefully, the steps, the one or two hogsheads, but no sign did they reveal.

"It gets me," said Tom, as they sat down on the edge of the platform, dangling their legs.

"He swore he wouldn't go near a railroad—remember?" said Roy, smiling a little wistfully.

Tom slowly shook his head.

"It's all my fault," said Roy.

"Meanwhile, we're losing time," said Tom.

"You don't suppose—" began Roy. "Where do you suppose that freight stopped? Here?"

Tom said nothing for a few moments. Then he jumped down and kneeling with his light began again examining the confusion of footprints near the siding. Roy watched him eagerly. He felt guilty and discouraged. Tom was apparently absorbed with some fresh thought. Around one footprint he drew a ring in the soil. Then he got up and crept along by the rail throwing his light upon it. About twelve or fifteen feet along this he paused, and crossing suddenly, examined the companion rail exactly opposite. Then he straightened up.

Percy K. Fitzhugh

"What is it?" asked Roy. But he got no answer.

Tom went back along the rail till he came to a point twelve or fifteen feet in the other direction from the group of footprints, and here he made another careful scrutiny of both rails. The group of footprints was outside the track and midway between the two points in which he seemed so much interested.

"This is the end of *our* tracking," he said at length.

"What's the matter?"

"Come here and I'll show you. See that footprint—it's only half a one—the front half—see? That's the last one of the lot. That's where he climbed into the car—see?"

Roy stood speechless.

"See? Now come here and I'll show you something. See those little rusty places on the track? It's fresh rust—see? You can wipe it off with your finger. There's where the wheels were—see? One, two, three, four—same on the other side, see? And down there," pointing along the track, "it's the same way. If it hadn't been raining this week, we'd never known about a freight car being stalled here, hey? See, those footprints are just half-way between the rusty spots. There's where the door was. See? This little front half of a footprint tells the story. He had to climb to get in—poor kid. He went on a railroad train, after all."

Roy could say nothing. He could only stare as Tom pointed here and there and fitted things together like a picture puzzle. The car was gone, but it had left its marks, just as the boy had.

"You put it into my head when you mentioned the train," said Tom.

"Oh, sure; *I* put it into your head," said Roy, in disgust. "*I'm* a wonderful scout—*I* ought to have a tin medal! It was you brought me that letter back. It was Pee-wee got the bird down and won a boat for us—and I've turned him out of it," he added, bitterly.

"No, you—"

"Yes, I have. And it was *you* that tracked him, and it was *you* spelled this out and it's *you*—it's just like *you*, too—to turn around and say I put it into your head. The only thing *I've* done in this whole blooming business is try to insult Mary Temple—only—only you wouldn't let me get away with it," he stammered.

"Roy," interrupted Tom, "listen—just a minute." He had never seen Roy like this before.

"Come on," said Roy, sharply. "You've done all *you* could. Come on back!"

Tom was not much at talking, but seeing his friend in this state seemed to give him words and he spoke earnestly and with a depth of feeling.

"It's always *you*," said Roy. "It's—"

"Roy," said Tom, "don't—wait a minute—*please*. When we got back to the boat I said we'd have to find him—don't go on like that, Roy—please! I thought I could find him. But you see I can't—*I* can't find him."

"You can make these tracks talk to you. I'm a—"

"No, you're not; listen, *please*. I said—you remember how I said I wanted to be alone with you—you remember? Well, now we are alone, and it's going to be you to do it, Roy; it's going to be *you* to bring Pee-wee back. Just the same as you made me a scout a year ago, you remember? You're the only one can do it, Roy," he put his hand on Roy's shoulder, "and I'll—I'll help you. And it'll seem like old times—sort of— Roy. But you're the one to do it. You haven't forgotten about the searchlight, have you, Roy? You remember how you told me about the scout's arm having a long reach? You remember, Roy? Come on, hurry up!"

CHAPTER XII

THE LONG ARM OF THE SCOUT

As Tom spoke, there came rushing into Roy's memory as vivid as the searchlight's shaft, a certain dark night a year before when Tom Slade, hoodlum, had stood by his side and with eyes of wonder watched him flash a message from Blakeley's Hill to the city below to undo a piece of vicious mischief of which Tom had been guilty. He had turned the heavens into an open book for Westy Martin, miles away, to read what he should do.

A thrill of new hope seized Roy.

"So you see it *will* be you, Roy."

"It has to be you to remind me of it."

"Shut up!" said Tom.

They ran for the boat at top speed, for, as they both realized, it was largely a fight against time.

"That train was dragging along pretty slow when it passed *us*," said Tom.

Percy K. Fitzhugh

"Sure, 'bout a million cars," Roy panted. "There's an up-grade, too, I think, between here and Poughkeepsie. Be half an hour, anyway, before they make it. You're a wonder. We'll kid the life out of Pee-wee for riding on a train after all. 'Spose he did it on purpose or got locked in?"

"Locked in, I guess," said Tom. "Let's try scout pace, I'm getting winded."

The searchlight which had been an important adjunct of the old *Nymph* had not been used on the *Good Turn*, for the reason that the boys had not run her at night. It was an acetylene light of splendid power and many a little craft Harry Stanton had picked up with it in his nocturnal cruising. Pee-wee had polished its reflector one day to pass the time, but with the exception of that attention it had lain in one of the lockers.

Reaching the boat they pulled the light out, connected it up, and found to their delight that it was in good working order.

"My idea," said Roy, now all excitement, "is to flash it from that hill, then from the middle of the river. Of course, it's a good deal a question of luck, but it seems as if *somebody* ought to catch it, in all these places along the river. Be great if we could find him to-night, hey?"

"They'd just have to hold him till we could get there in the boat—they couldn't get him back here."

"No sooner said than stung," said Roy; "hurry up, bring that can, and some matches and—yes, you might as well bring the Manual anyway, thought I know that code backwards."

"You're right you do," said Tom.

He was glad to see Roy himself again and taking the lead, as usual.

"If there was only one of these telegraph operators—guys, as I used to call them—star-gazing, we'd pass the word to him, all right."

"A word to the guys, hey? Come on, hustle!"

A strenuous climb brought them to the brow of a hill from which the lights of several villages, and the more numerous lights of Poughkeepsie could be seen.

"Now, Tomasso, see-a if you know-a de lesson—queeck! Connect that up and—look out you don't step on the tube! I wish we had a pedestal or something. When you're roaming, you have to do as the Romans do, hey? Open your Manual to page 232. No!" he said hurriedly looking over Tom's shoulder. "*Care of the fingernails!* That's *259* you've got. What do you think we're going to do, start a manicure parlor? *There* you are—now keep the place to make assurance doubly sure. Here goes! Hello, folks!" he called, as he swung the long shaft fan-wise across the heavens. "Now, three dots for S?"

"Right," said Tom.

Roy sent three short flashes into the night, then paused and sent a longer flash of about three seconds. Another pause, then three of the longer flashes, then a short one, two long ones and a short one.

"S-T-O-P—stop," he said.

"Right-o," concurred Tom.

"Now F—two shorts, a long and a short—is it?"

"You know blamed well it is," said Tom.

Thus the message was sent.

"Stop freight going north; boy locked in car. Hold. Friends coming up river in boat flying yellow flag."

They had on board a large yellow flag with TEMPLE CAMP on it, and Roy thought of this as being the best means of identifying the boat for anyone who might be watching for it along the shore.

Three times they flashed the message, then hurried back to the boat and chugged out, anchoring in midstream. The course of the river is as straight as an arrow here. The lights in the small towns of Milton and Camelot were visible on either side; tiny lights flickered along the railroads that skirted either shore, and beyond in the distance twinkled the lights on the great bridge at Poughkeepsie.

"We're right in the steamer's path here," said Tom; "let's hurry."

Roy played the shaft for a minute to attract attention, then threw his message again and again into the skies. The long, bright, silent column seemed to fill the whole heaven as it pierced the darkness in short and long flashes. The chugging of the *Good Turn's* engine was emphasized by the solemn stillness as they ran in toward shore, and the splash of their dropping anchor awakened a faint echo from the neighboring mountains.

"Well, that's all we can do till morning," said Roy. "What do you say to some eats?"

"Gee, it's big and wild and lonely, isn't it?" said Tom.

They had never thought of the Hudson in this way before.

After breakfast in the morning they started upstream, their big yellow camp flag flying and keeping as near the shore as possible so as to be within hail. Now that the black background of the night had passed and the broad daylight was all about them, their hope had begun to wane. The spell seemed broken; the cheerful reality of the morning sunlight upon the water and the hills seemed to dissipate their confidence in that long shaft, and they saw the whole experience of the night as a sort of fantastic dream.

But Pee-wee was gone; there was no dream about that, and the boat did not seem like the same place without him.

The first place they passed was Stoneco, but there was no sign of life near the shore, and the *Good Turn* chugged by unheeded. They ran across to Milton where a couple of men lolled on a wharf and a few people were waiting at the little station. They could not get in very close to the shore on account of the flats, but Roy, making a megaphone of an old newspaper, asked if a flash message had been received there. After much shouting back and forth, he learned that the searchlight had been seen but had been thought to be from one of the night boats plying up and down the river. It had evidently meant nothing to the speaker or to anyone else there. Roy asked if they would please ask the telegraph operator if he had seen it.

"He'd understand it all right," he said, a bit disheartened. But the answer came back that the operator had not seen it.

At Poughkeepsie they made a landing at the wharf. Here expressmen were moving trunks about, a few stragglers waiting for some boat peered through the gates like prisoners; there was a general air of bustle and a "city" atmosphere about the place. A few people gathered about, looking at the *Good Turn* and watching the boys as they made their way up the wharf.

"Boy Scouts," they heard someone say.

There was the usual good-natured curiosity which follows scouts when they are away from home and which they have come to regard as a matter of course, but the big yellow flag seemed to carry no particular meaning to anyone here.

They walked up to the station where they asked the operator if he had seen the searchlight message or heard anything about it, but he had not. They inquired who was the night watchman on the wharf, hunted him out, and asked him. He had seen the light and wondered what and where it was. That was all.

"Foiled again!" said Roy.

They made inquiries of almost everyone they saw, going into a nearby hotel and several of the stores. They inquired at the fire house, where they thought men would have been up at night who might be expected to know the Morse code, but the spokesman there shook his head.

"A fellow who was with us got locked in a freight car," Roy explained, "and we signaled to people up this way to stop the train."

The man smiled; apparently he did not take Roy's explanation very seriously. "Now if you could only get that convict that escaped down yonder—"

"We have no interest in him," said Roy, shortly.

He and Tom had both counted on Poughkeepsie with its police force and fire department and general wide-awakeness, and they went back to the *Good Turn* pretty well discouraged, particularly as the good people of whom they had inquired had treated them with an air of kindly indulgence, smiling at their story, saying that the scouts were a wide-awake lot, and so forth; interested, but good-naturedly skeptical. One had said, "Are you making believe to telegraph that way? Well, it's good fun, anyway." Another asked if they had been reading dime novels. The patronizing tone had rather nettled the boys.

"I'd like to have told that fellow that if we *had* been reading dime novels, we wouldn't have had time to learn the Morse code," said Roy.

"The Motor Boat Heroes!" mocked Tom.

"Yes, volume three thousand, and they haven't learned how to run a gas engine yet! Get out your magnifying glass, Tom; what's that, a village, up there?"

"A house."

"Some house, too," said Roy, looking at the diminutive structure near the shore. "Put your hand down the chimney and open the front door, hey?"

But as they ran in nearer the shore other houses showed themselves around the edge of the hill and here, too, was a little wharf with several people upon it and near it, on the shore, a surging crowd on the edge of which stood several wagons.

Percy K. Fitzhugh

"Guess they must be having a mass meeting about putting a new spring on the post-office door," said Roy. "Somebody ought to lay a paperweight on that village a windy day like this. It might blow away. Close your throttle a little, Tom and put your timer back; we'll run in and see what's up."

"You don't suppose all that fuss can have anything to do with Pee-wee, do you?" Tom asked.

"No, it looks more as if a German submarine had landed there. There wouldn't be so much of a rumpus if they'd got the kid."

But in another moment Roy's skeptical mood had changed as he saw a tall, slender fellow in brown standing at the end of the wharf with arms outspread.

"What's he doing—posing for the movies?"

"He's semaphoring," Tom answered.

"I'll be jiggered if he isn't!" said Roy, all interest at once. "C—O—M—E—I—(he makes his I too much like his C)— N. *What do you know about that!* Come in!"

The stranger held what seemed to be a large white placard in either hand in place of a flag and his motions were not as clear-cut as they should have been, but to Roy, with whom, as he had often said, the semaphore code was like "pumpkin pie," the message was plain.

As they ran alongside the wharf the khaki-clad signaler greeted them with the scout salute.

"Pretty brisk out on the water this morning?" he said. "We got your message—we were out canoeing last night; you use the International code, don't you?"

"Have you got him?" Roy asked anxiously.

"Oh, yes, he's here; pulled in somewhere around midnight, I guess. He stayed all night with one of our troop; he's up there now getting his breakfast. Great kid, isn't he?" he laughed. "He was telling us about rice cakes. We're kind of out of date up here, you know. I was a little balled up on your spacing," he added as they went up the wharf. "I haven't got the International down very good. Yes, we were drifting around, a couple of us, telling Ford jokes, when you sprung it on us."

"Have you got the signaling badge?" said Roy.

"Oh, yes, I managed to pull that; I'm out for the star now."

"You'll get it," said Tom.

"Is the kid all right?" Roy asked.

"Oh, sure; but he had some pretty rough handling, I guess. It was quite a little movie show when we dragged the other one out. Lucky the station agent and the constable were there. He's up there now waiting for the men from Ossining."

Through the surging crowd Tom and Roy could see, sitting on a bench at the station, a man in convict garb, with his hands manacled together and a guard on either side of him. In the broad light of day he was a desperate-looking creature, as he sat with his ugly head hanging low, apparently oblivious to all about him.

"I don't understand," said Roy.

"Didn't you know about him?"

"Not a thing—except we did know someone got away from Sing Sing the other night—but we never thought—"

"Didn't you know he was in the same car? That's why the little fellow couldn't get away. He'd have come back to you, sure."

Roy doubted it, but he said nothing and presently the mystery was cleared up by the arrival on the scene of Pee-wee himself, accompanied by several scouts. They were laughing merrily and seemed greatly elated that the boat had come; but Pee-wee was rather embarrassed and held back until Roy dragged him forward.

"Kiddo," said he, looking straight into the boy's face, "the *Good Turn* couldn't have lived another day without you. So you did hit the railroad after all, didn't you? Gee, it's good to see you; you've caused us more worry—" he put his arm over Pee-wee's shoulder and turned away with him, and the others, being good scouts, had sense enough not to follow.

"Pee-wee," said Roy, "don't try to tell me—that can wait. Listen, kiddo. We're in the same boat, you and I. We each wrote a letter that we shouldn't have written, but yours was received and mine wasn't—thanks to Tom. We've got to forget about both those letters, Pee-wee. I was ashamed of mine before I'd finished writing it. There's no good talking about it now. You're with us because we want you with us, not because Mary Temple wanted it, but because *I* want you and Tom wants you; do you hear? You know who it is that's always doing something for someone and never getting any credit for it, don't you? It's Tom Slade. He saved me from being a crazy fool—from sending that letter to Mary. And I came to my senses the next day. He tracked you to that car, only it always seems to work around so that someone else gets all the glory. It makes me feel like a—Listen to them over there now, talking about *signaling*. Pee-wee, you gave us an awful scare. It didn't seem natural on top of the cabin last night without you—you little mascot! We're not going to have another word to say about this, kid—I'm your patrol leader, remember. We're going to hit it straight for camp now—the three of us—the Big Three—and you're with us because we can't do without you. Do you get that?"

"Roy," said Pee-wee, speaking with difficulty. "I—I had an—adventure."

"Well, I should think you did."

CHAPTER XIII

TEMPLE CAMP

The scouts of the village stood upon the wharf and waved a last good-bye to the three as the *Good Turn* chugged merrily away.

"I'm going to give that fellow the full salute," said Tom, raising his hand to his forehead. "He's a wonder."

The scouts on shore received this tribute to their comrade with shouts, throwing their hats in the air and giving three lusty cheers for the "Silver Foxes and the Elks" as the launch, swerving out into midstream, bent her course for Catskill Landing.

"He sure is a wonder," said Roy.

"I told him all about you," chimed in Pee-wee, "and all the stunts you can do."

"He seems to be prouder of his Ford jokes than of his signal work," laughed Roy. "He—"

"Oh, crinkums, he knows some dandy Ford jokes, and his wrist is so strong from paddling that he can stick a shovel in the ground and turn it around with one hand; oh, he's got that paddle twist down fine, Roy; but, gee, he says you're all right; even before you came he said that; as soon as I told him who it was that signaled—"

"Do you think they'll come up?" Roy interrupted.

"Sure they will; I told them all about the camp and how they could have a cabin to themselves—they're only a small troop, one patrol, and he wants to know you better; gee, I told him all about you and how you could—"

"All right, kiddo," laughed Roy.

"They're coming up in August. Say, that fellow's got eleven merit badges, but the one thing he's crazy to get is the gold cross."

"He'll get it," said Tom, who had been wiping the engine.

"He says the trouble is," added Pee-wee, "that he can't save anybody's life with great danger to his own—that's what it says in the Manual, isn't it?"

"Yes," said Tom, quietly.

"He says the trouble is nobody ever gets in danger. The trouble with his troop is they all know how to swim and they're so blamed clever that he never has a chance to rescue one of them. He said he tipped the canoe over with one fellow and the fellow just wouldn't be saved; he swam around and dived and wouldn't let Garry imperil his life— and that's the only way you can do it, Roy. You've got to imperil your own life, and he says he never gets a chance to imperil his life."

Percy K. Fitzhugh

"Must be discouraging," said Roy.

"Oh, jiminys, you'd laugh to hear him talk; he's got that quiet way about him, Roy—sober like. I told him there's lots of different ways a feller can imperil his life."

"Sure, fifty-seven varieties," said Roy. "Well, I'm glad they treated you so well, kid, and I hope we'll have a chance to pay them back. What do you say we tie up in Kingston and have a soda?"

Early the next day they came in sight of Catskill Landing. Roy stood on top of the cabin like Columbus, his rapt gaze fixed upon the dock.

"We have arrove," said he. "Gee, I'm sorry it's over."

The trip *had* been enjoyable, but now their every thought was centered upon Temple Camp to which they were so near and they were filled with delightful anticipations as they made ready for the hike which still lay before them. The boating club, with the hospitality which a love of the water seems always to inspire in its devotees, gave them a mooring buoy and from this, having made their boat fast, they rowed ashore and set out with staves and duffel bags for the quaint little village of Leeds.

The distance to Leeds depends upon who is making the journey, or from whom you get your information. The farmers will tell you it is five miles. The summer boarders are likely to tell you that it is ten. To be exact, it is somewhere between two miles and twenty miles, and you can't get back to Catskill Landing for dinner.

"I think it's ten miles there and twenty miles back," said Roy; "*we* should worry! When we get to Leeds we make our grand dash for the lake."

"Like Peary," said Pee-wee, already bubbling over with excitement.

"Something like him, yes."

Their way took them through a beautiful hilly country and for a while they had glimpses of the river, which brought them pleasant reminiscences of their rambling, happy-go-lucky voyage.

"Who does the *Good Turn* belong to?" Tom asked.

"I think it belongs to Honorable Pee-wee Harris," said Roy. "He did the trick that won it."

"I'll tell you who she belongs to," said Pee-wee. "She belongs to the First Bridgeboro Troop, Boy Scouts of America."

"Raven, Fox and Elk!" said Roy. "Right you are, Pee-wee. United we stand, divided we squall."

A tramp of a couple of hours over country roads brought them to Leeds, and they hiked along its main street contributing not a little to its picturesqueness with their alert, jaunty air, their brown complexions which matched so well with the scout attire, their duffel bags and their long staves. More than one farmer and many an early summer boarder stared at them and hailed them pleasantly as they passed along.

"I like this village," said Pee-wee.

"I'll have it wrapped up for you," said Roy; "Take it, or have

Percy K. Fitzhugh

it sent?"

"How do we get to Black Lake?" Tom asked of a man who was lounging outside one of the shops.

"Ye ain't goin' to walk it, be ye?" he answered, scrutinizing them curiously.

"Right you are," said Roy. "How did you guess?"

"Ye got a pooty smart walk afore ye," the man said, dubiously.

"Well, we're pretty smart boys," said Roy. "Break it to us gently, and let us hear the worst."

"Baout five mile 'f ye take th' hill rud."

"Gracious, goodness me!" said Roy, "are they all the same length?"

"Haouw?"

"The miles; lads, I'm just reckless enough to do it."

"Wall," drawled their informant, "Ye go 'long this rud t'l ye come t' a field whar thar's a red caouw, then ye cut right through th' middle uv it 'n' go on over a stun wall 'n' ye'll come to a woods rud. Ye foller that t'l ye come to a side path on the left on it that goes up hill. Black Lake's t'other side that hill. Ye got to pick yer way up through the woods 'long that path if ye kin foller it, 'n' when ye git t' the top ye kin look daown 'n' see th' lake, but ye'll have a smart climb gettin' daown th' hill."

"That's us," said Roy. "Thanks—thanks very much."

When they had gone a little way he halted Tom and Pee-wee with a dramatic air.

"Lads," said he, "we've got the *Motor Boat Heroes* and the *Dauntless Chums* and *Submarine Sam* beaten to a frazzle! We're the *Terrible Trio Series*, volume two million. Lads, get out your dirks and keep up stout hearts. We have to cut through the middle of a red cow! That man said so!"

Three-quarters of an hour more along an apparently disused road and they came upon a trail which was barely discernible, leading up a steep and densely wooded hill. In places they had to climb over rugged terraces, extricating themselves from such mazes of tangled underbrush as they had never before seen. Now and then the path seemed to peter out and they found it again with difficulty and only by the skilful use of scout tracking lore. The long, steep climb was filled with difficulties, but they pressed on amazed at the wildness all about them.

At last, by dint of much hard effort and after many wasted steps through loss of the trail, they came out upon the summit, and looked down upon a sight which sent a thrill to all three. The other side of the hill was, perhaps, not as steep as the side which they had mounted, but it was thickly wooded and at its base was a sheet of water surrounded by lofty hills, all covered with dense forest, which extended right down to the water's edge. The lake was perhaps a mile long, and lay like a dark jewel amid the frowning heights which closed it in. The trees along shore were dimly reflected in the still, black water. The quiet of the spot was intense. It was relieved by no sign of habitation, save a little thin, uncertain column of smoke which rose from among the trees on the farther shore.

The solemnity of the scene, the blackness and isolation of

that sheet of water, the dense woods, rising all around it and shutting out the world, was quite enough to cast a spell on anyone, and the three boys looked about them awestruck and for a moment speechless.

"Jiminy crinkums!" said Pee-wee, at length.

Tom only shook his head.

"Reminds you of Broadway and Forty-second Street," said Roy.

They started down the hill and found that their descent was quite as difficult as the ascent had been, but at last they reached the foot and now, from this lower viewpoint they could catch a glimpse of the wood interior on the opposite shore. There were several log cabins harmonizing in color with the surrounding forest and, therefore, inconspicuous. Farther from the shore the boys glimpsed another and larger structure and at the water's edge they now saw a boat drawn up.

It was evident that the way they had come was not the usual way to reach the camp, for there was no sign of trail along the shore, and to pick their way around, with the innumerable obstacles which beset the way, would have taken several hours.

"It must be lively around here on Saturday nights with the crowd out doing their marketing, and the movie shows—" began Roy.

"Aw, shut up!" said Pee-wee.

They raised their voices in unison and shouted, and the echo resounded from the hills across the water, almost as loud and distinguishable as their own call. Roy yelled long and loud, slapping his open lips with the palm of his hand, and a pandemonium of similar sounds came back as if from a multitude of voices.

"I tell you, when John Temple does a thing he does it right!" said Pee-wee. "Gee, you can't deny that!"

In a few moments a man approached on the opposite shore and leisurely got into the boat. As he rowed across, he looked around once in a while, and as the boat drew near the boys saw that its occupant had iron gray hair, a long drooping moustache, and a face deeply wrinkled and browned almost to a mulatto hue.

"Hello," called Roy. "Is that Temple Camp over there? I guess we came in the back way."

"Thet's it," said the man. "You some o' the Bridgeboro boys?"

His voice was low and soft, as of one who has lived long in the woods by himself. There was a humorous twinkle in his eye which the boys liked. He was long and lanky and wore khaki trousers and a coarse gray flannel shirt. His arms, which were bare, were very sinewy. Altogether, the impression which he made on the boys was that he was perfectly self-possessed and at ease, so absolutely sure of himself that nothing in all the wide world could frighten him or disconcert him. The President of the United States, kings, emperors, millionaires—including John Temple—might want to be rowed across and this man would come leisurely over and get them, but he would not hurry and he would be no more embarrassed or flustered at meeting them than a tree would be. Nature, the woods and mountains and prairies, had put their stamp upon him, had whispered their secrets to him, and civilization could not phase him. That was the way he struck the boys, who from being scouts had learned to be observant and discerning.

"Are you Mr. Rushmore?" Tom asked, and as the man nodded assent he continued, "My name is Tom Slade; we're members of the Bridgeboro Troop and I'm the one selected to help you. I don't know if you expected me yet, but my scoutmaster and Mr. Temple thought I better come ahead of the other fellows so's to help you and get acquainted—like. These fellows came with me just for fun, but, of course, they want to help get things ready. The rest are coming up in July."

This was a good deal for Tom to say at a stretch, and it fell to the voluble Pee-wee later to edify Mr. Rushmore with all the details of their trip, winding up with a glowing peroration on Roy's greatness.

"Waal, I reck'n I'm glad ye've come—the hull three on ye," Jeb Rushmore drawled.

"That's some trail over that hill," said Roy, as they rowed across. "We lost it about a dozen times."

"Thet? Thet ain't no trail," said Jeb. "Thet's a street—a thurafare. I'm a-goin' t' test you youngsters out follerin' thet on a dark night."

"Have a heart!" said Roy. "I could never pick that out with a flashlight."

"A what? Ye won't hev no light o' no sort, not ef *I* know it."

The boys laughed. "Well, I see we're up against the real thing," said Roy, "but if that's a thoroughfare, I'd like to see a trail—that's all."

"Ye don' need ter see it," drawled Jeb. "Ye jest *feel* it."

"You must have a pretty good sense of touch," said Roy.

"Ye don' feel it with your hands, youngster, ye jest *sense* it."

"*Good night!*" said Roy.

Tom said nothing. He had been watching Mr. Rushmore and hanging with rapt attention on his every word.

They found the hill on the opposite shore not as steep as it had looked from across the water, and here at its base, in the dim solitude by the shore, was Temple Camp. There was a large open pavilion built of untrimmed wood, which would accommodate eight or ten troops, allowing to each some measure of privacy and there were as many as a dozen log cabins, some large enough for two or three patrols, others intended evidently to accommodate but one. There was a shack for the storage of provisions and equipment, in which the boys saw among other things piles upon piles of wooden platters.

"Not much dishwashing here," said Pee-wee, joyfully.

Here, also, were half a dozen tents and every imaginable article necessary to camp life. Close by was a cooking shack and outside this several long mess boards with rough seats; and just beyond was a spring of clear water.

Jeb Rushmore had a cabin to himself upon the outside of which sprawled the skins of as many as a dozen different sorts of animals—the trophies of his life in the West.

John Temple had certainly done the thing right; there was no doubt of that. He had been a long time falling, but when he fell he fell hard. Temple Camp comprised one hundred acres of woodland—"plenty of room to grow in," as Jeb said. It was more than a camp; it was really a community, and had somewhat the appearance of a frontier trading post. In its construction very little bark had been taken from the wood; the whole collection of buildings fitted well in their wild surroundings; there wasn't a jarring note.

But Temple Camp was unique not only in its extent, its rustic character and its magnificent situation; it was the fulfilment of a grand dream which John Temple had dreamed. Any troop of scouts could, by making timely application to the trustees, go to Temple Camp and remain three weeks without so much as a cent of cost. There was to be absolutely no favoritism of any kind (and Jeb Rushmore was the man to see to that), not even in the case of the Bridgeboro Troop; except that troops from cities were to be given preference over troops from country districts. Jeb Rushmore was to be the camp manager, working with the trustees and the visiting scoutmasters; but as it turned out he became a character in this scout village, and if he fell short in executive capacity he more than made up for it in other ways. Before the first season was over people came miles to see him. There were also a doctor and a cook, though a troop occupying a cabin could do its own cooking and mess by itself if it chose.

There were some rather interesting rules and regulations. If a scout won a merit badge while at camp this entitled his whole troop to lengthen its stay by two days, if it so elected. If he won the life scout badge, four extra days was the reward of his whole troop. The star badge meant an extra week, the eagle badge ten extra days. A scout winning the bronze cross was entitled with his troop to occupy "Hero Cabin" and to remain two extra weeks at camp. The silver cross meant three extra weeks; the gold cross four extra weeks. If a troop could not conveniently avail itself of this extra time privilege in the current season it could be credited with the time and use it, whole or piecemeal, in subsequent seasons.

On the lake there were to be several boats which were not yet ready, and every scout winning a life saving medal was to have a boat named for him. At the time the boys arrived there was only one boat and that was named *Mary Temple*.

CHAPTER XIV

HERO CABIN

The history of Temple Camp during that gala season of its opening would fill a book; but this is not a history of Temple Camp, and we must pass at once to those extraordinary happenings which shook the little scout community to its very center and cast a shadow over the otherwise pleasant and fraternal life there.

By the middle of July every inch of space in the pavilion was occupied, and among the other troops which lodged there was the little troop from down the Hudson, of which Garry Everson was the leader. Tom had tried to procure cabin accommodations for these good friends, but the cabins had all been spoken for before their application came and they had to be content with the less desirable quarters. During the early days of their stay the Bridgeboro Troop arrived in a blaze of glory; the Ravens, with their pride and delight, Doc Carson, first aid boy; the rest of the Silver Foxes with Westy Martin, Dorry Benton and others; and Tom's own patrol, the Elks, with Connie Bennett, the Bronson boys, the famous O'Connor twins, all with brand new outfits, for this was a new patrol. Three small cabins had been reserved for them and in these they settled down, each patrol by itself and flying its own flag. Tom, by reason of his duties, which identified him with the camp as a whole rather than with any troop or patrol, occupied the cabin with Jeb Rushmore, and though he was much with the Elks, he had delegated Connie Bennett to substitute as patrol leader for the time being.

Garry Everson was a general favorite. Not only had his stunt of receiving the signal message and restoring the fugitive Pee-wee won him high regard with the Bridgeboro boys, but his quiet manner and whimsical humor had made him many friends throughout the camp. He was tall and slim, but muscular; the water seemed to be his specialty; he was an expert at rowing and paddling, he could dive in a dozen different ways and as for swimming, no one at Temple Camp could begin to compete with him.

Tom's friendship with Garry Everson had grown quite intimate. They were both interested in tracking and made many little trips together, for Tom had much time to himself.

One morning, as Tom, according to rule, was making his regular inspection of the pavilion, he lingered for a few minutes in Garry's corner to chat with him.

"You're not getting ready to go?" he asked in surprise, noticing that some of the troop's paraphernalia had been packed.

"Beginning to get ready," said Garry. "Sit down. Why didn't you bring your knitting?"

"I can't stay long," said Tom. "I've got to inspect the cabins yet, and then I've got to make up the program for campfire yarns to-night. By the way, couldn't *you* give us a spiel?"

"Oh, sure," said Garry. "*The Quest of the Honor Medal.* I'll tell how nobody ever gets into danger here—or imperils his life, as Pee-wee would say. I'm going to put a notice up on one of the trees and get you to read another at mess with the regular announcements: Wanted; by scout seeking honor medal; someone willing to imperil his life. Suitable reward. Apply Temple Camp pavilion. Signed, Would-be Hero."

Tom laughed.

"I'm like old What's-his-name, Caesar. Ready to do the conquest act, but nothing more to conquer. Believe me, it's no cinch being a would-be hero. Couldn't you get bitten by a rattlesnake on one of your tracking stunts? Get your foot on him, you know, and he'll be wriggling and squirming to get his head free, and his cruel fangs will be within an inch of your ankle and you'll just begin to feel them against your stocking—"

"Don't," laughed Tom.

"When all of a sudden I'll come bounding out of the thicket, and I'll grab him by the head and force his cruel jaws shut and slip an elastic band around his mug. That ought to pull the silver cross, hey? And I and my faithful followers would get three extra weeks in camp."

"Would you like to stay longer?" Tom asked.

"Foolish question, number three million. Haven't we had the time of our young lives? I never knew two weeks to go so fast. Never mind, we've got two days more—and two days *only* unless I get some answers to my 'ad.'"

"Where's your patrol this morning?"

"Stalking; they've a date with a robin. I would have gone along except I didn't see much chance of any of them imperilling their lives taking snapshots of robins. So I stayed home to do a little packing—things we won't need again. But no use thinking about that, I suppose; that's what I tell them. We've had some good times, all right. Seems a pity we have to go just when Mr. Temple and his daughter have come. You're a lucky kid; you stay till the last gun is fired, don't you?"

"Yes, I'm going to stay till we close up. Come on, stroll up the hill with me. I've got to raise the colors. If you've only two days more there's no use moping around in here."

"All right, wait a minute and I'll be with you—dry the pensive tear, as your friend Roy would say. He's an all-around scout, isn't he?"

"Yes, he came right off the cover of the Manual, Mr. Ellsworth says."

"You're a bully troop, you fellows. Gee, I envy you. Trouble with us," he continued, as they walked up the hill together, "is we haven't any scoutmaster. I'm scoutmaster and patrol leader rolled into one. We're going to get better organized this winter. There's only just the seven of us, you know, and we haven't got any money. You might think that because we live in a country village on the Hudson everything's fine and dandy. But there's blamed little money in our burg. Four of our troop have to work after school. One works all day and goes to night school down to Poughkeepsie. I saved up two years to buy that canoe I was in when I caught your message."

"Well, you caught it all right," said Tom, with a note of pride in his usually expressionless voice.

"We'll come out all right, though," said Garry, cheerily.

"That's what I'm always telling them; only we're so gol-blamed poor."

"I know what it is," said Tom, after a pause. "Maybe that's what makes us such good friends, sort of. I lived in a tenement down in Bridgeboro. I've got to thank Roy for everything—Roy and Mr. Ellsworth. They all treat me fine and you'd never know most of them are rich fellows; but somehow—I don't just know how to tell you—but you know how a scout is supposed to be a brother to every other scout. Well, it seems to me, kind of, as if a poor fellow is a brother to every other poor fellow—and—and—I understand."

"It's easy to see they all think a lot of you," said Garry. "Well, we've had a rattling good time up here and I don't suppose we'll feel any worse about going away than lots of others will. If you miss one thing you usually have another to make up. We're all good friends in our little troop—we have more fun than you could shake a stick at, joshing each other about different kinds of heroic stunts, to win an honor medal, and some of them have thought up the craziest things—"

"I wish you could stay," said Tom.

"Well, if wishes were horses, beggars would ride, as some old duffer said."

The wooded hill sloped upward behind the camp for a distance of some hundred yards, where it was broken by a sheer precipice forming one side of a deep gully. This was the work of man, having once been a railroad cut, but it had been in disuse for many years and was now covered with vegetation. You could walk up the hill till you came to the brink of this almost vertical chasm, but you could no more scramble down it than you could scramble down a well. On the opposite side of the cut the hill continued upward and the bridging of the chasm by the scouts themselves had been a subject of much discussion; but up to the present time nothing had been done and there was no way to continue one's ascent of the hill except to follow along the edge of the cut to a point where the precipice was low enough to allow one to scramble down—a walk of several miles.

Right on the brink of this old overgrown cut was a shack which had probably once been used by the workmen. Although on the Camp property it was rather too far removed from the other buildings to be altogether convenient as a living place, but its isolated situation had attracted the boys, and the idea of calling it Hero Cabin was an inspiration of Roy's. Mr. Keller, one of the trustees, had fallen in with the notion and while deprecating the use of this remote shack for regular living quarters, had good-naturedly given his consent that it be used as the honored domicile of any troop a member of which had won an honor medal. Perhaps he thought that, honor medals being not so easily won, it would be quite safe to make this concession.

In any event, it was quite enough for the boys. A committee was formed with a member from each troop to make the shack a suitable abode for a hero and his court. Impulsive Roy was the moving spirit of the plan; Pee-wee was its megaphone, and in the early days of the Bridgeboro troop's stay a dozen or more scouts had worked like beavers making a path up through the woods, covering the shack with bark, and raising a flagpole near it. They had hiked into Leeds and bought material for a flag to fly above the shack showing the name, HERO CABIN, and they had fitted it with rustic bunks inside.

The idea was a good one, the boys had taken a great deal of pride and pleasure in the work of preparation, the whole thing had given rise to much friendly jealousy as to what troop should be honored by residence here and what fortunate scout should be escorted to this new abode amid acclamations. Probably every troop in camp had dreams of occupying it (I am sure that Pee-wee had), and of spending its "honor time" here.

But apparently Mr. Keller, who was not much given to dreaming, was right in his skeptical conjecture for Hero Cabin remained unoccupied, though Tom made it a point to tramp up and raise and lower the colors there each day.

"Some day, maybe next season," said he as they stood on the brink and gazed across the deep gully, "they'll bring somebody up here riding on their shoulders. You can't win an honor medal every day in the week. I think the bronze cross would be enough for *me*—let alone the silver or the gold one. I'd be satisfied with that, wouldn't you?"

"Except that the gold cross gives you four extra weeks," said Garry, "and, of course, the more risk a fellow takes, the greater the honor is." He picked up a pebble and threw it at a tree across the gully. "I'd rather have one of those medals," he said, "than anything in the world—and I want a wireless outfit pretty bad, too. But besides that" (he kept throwing pebbles across the gully and spoke half absently), "besides that, it would be fine to have that extra time. Maybe we couldn't use it *all* this season, but—look, I can hit that thin tree every time—but I'm thinking of the little codger mostly; you know the one I mean—with the light hair?"

"The little fellow that coughs?"

"He doesn't cough any more. He did before we came up here. His father died of consumption. No, he doesn't cough much now—guess it agrees with him up here. He's—There, I hit it six times in succession."

For a few minutes Tom said nothing, but watched as Garry, time after time, hit the slender tree across the gully.

"I often dream about having an honor medal, too," he said, after a while. "We haven't got any in our troop. Roy'll be the one, I guess. I suppose the gold cross is the highest award they'll ever have, hey?"

"Guess so."

"There's nothing better than gold, is there?"

"It isn't because there's nothing better than gold," said Garry, still intent upon hitting his mark. "It's because there's nothing better than heroism—bravery—risking your life."

"Diamonds—they might have a diamond cross, hey?"

"What for?"

"In case they found anything that's better than heroism. [missing: "?]

"What?"

"Oh, I don't know. There might be."

Garry turned and laughingly clapped Tom on the back. "I might push you over this precipice and then jump down after you, hey?" he laughed.

"You'd be crushed to death yourself," said Tom.

"Well, stop talking nonsense or I'll do it. Come on, get your chores done and we'll go down and have a swim. What'd' you say?"

Percy K. Fitzhugh

He ran his hand through Tom's thick shock of hair and laughed again. "Come on, forget it," said he. "I've only got two days more here and I'm not going to miss a morning dip. Come on, I'll show you the double twist dive."

He put his arm through Tom's with the contagious gaiety that was his, and started down the hill with him toward the lake.

"Come on, wake up, you old grouch," he said.

CHAPTER XV

COWARD!

There were not many boys bathing at the time this thing happened. Roy and several of the Silver Foxes were at a little distance from the shore practising archery, and a number of scouts from other troops lolled about watching them. Three or four boys from a Pennsylvania troop were having an exciting time with the rowboat, diving from it out in the middle of the lake. Pee-wee Harris and Dory Bronson, of Tom's patrol, were taking turns diving from the spring-board. Tom and Garry joined them and, as usual, whenever Garry was diving, boys sauntered down to the shore and watched.

"Here goes the Temple Twist," said he, turning a complete somersault and then jerking himself sideways so as to strike the water crossways to the spring-board.

There was some applause as he came up spluttering. Tom tried it, but could not get the twist.

"Try this on your piano," said Garry, diving and striking the water flat.

"That's what you call the Bridgeboro Botch," he laughed, as Tom went sprawling into the water. "Hey, Blakeley," he shouted to Roy, "did you see the Bridgeboro Botch?"

"There's no use their trying *your* tricks," Roy called in genuine admiration. "I'm coming in in a few minutes, myself."

But Tom dived very well for all that, and so did Pee-wee, but Dory Bronson was new at the game.

The thing which was destined to have such far-reaching consequences happened suddenly and there was some difference of opinion among the eye-witnesses as to just how it occurred, but all were agreed as to the main fact. Dory had just dived, it was Pee-wee's turn next, Tom would follow, and then Garry, who meanwhile had stepped up to where Roy and the others were shooting, and was chatting with them.

They had dived in this order like clockwork for some time, so that when Dory did not appear on the board the others looked about for him. Just at that moment a piercing cry arose, and a dozen pairs of eyes were turned out on the lake where the boy was seen struggling frantically. It was evident that the boys in the boat were pulling to his assistance, but they were too far away and meanwhile he floundered and struggled like a madman, sending up cries that echoed from the hills. How he had gotten out so far no one knew, unless indeed he had tried to swim to the boat.

The sight of a human being struggling frantically in the water and lost to all sense of reason by panic fright is one to strike terror to a stout heart. Even the skilful swimmer whose courage is not of the stoutest may balk at the peril. That seemed to be the feeling which possessed Tom Slade as he stood upon the end of the spring-board and instead of diving cast a hurried look to where Garry Everson was talking with Roy.

It all happened in a moment, the cries from the lake, Tom's hesitation, his swift look toward Roy and Garry, and his evident relief as the latter rushed to the shore and plunged into the water. He stood there on the end of the high spring-board, conspicuous against the blue sky, with his eyes fixed upon the swimmer. He saw the struggle in the water, saw the frantic arms clutch at Garry, watched him as he extricated himself from that insane grasp, saw him catch the struggling figure with the "neck grip" as the only means of saving both lives, and watched him as he swam toward shore with his now almost unconscious burden. What he thought, how he felt, no human being knew. He stood motionless like a statue until the growing crowd below him set up a cheer. Then he went down and stood among them.

"Didn't you see him drowning there?" a fellow demanded of him.

"Yes, I did," said Tom.

The other stared at him for a moment with a peculiar expression, then swung on his heel and strode away.

Tom craned his neck to see and spoke to those nearest him, but they only answered perfunctorily or ignored him altogether. He moved around to where Roy stood, and Roy, without looking at him, pressed farther into the crowd.

"That's he," a boy near him whispered to his neighbor; "stood on the end of the board, watching. I didn't think we had any cowards here."

In every face and most of all in the faces of his own troop Tom saw contempt plainly written. He could not go away from them, for that might excite fresh comment; so he remained, trying to disregard the significant glances and swallowing hard to keep down the lump which kept rising in his throat.

Soon the doctor came, relieving Doc Carson of the Ravens, and the half-drowned boy was taken to his cabin.

"He—he's all right, isn't he?" Tom asked of the doctor.

"Yes," said the doctor, briefly. "He's one of your own patrol, isn't he?"

"Yes—sir."

The doctor looked at him for a moment and then turned away.

"Hello, old man," said Garry, as he passed him, hurrying to the pavilion. "Cold feet, eh? Guess you got a little rattled. Never mind."

The words stabbed Tom like a knife, but at least they were friendly and showed that Garry did not entirely condemn him.

He paused at the Elks cabin, the cabin of his own patrol, where most of the members of his troop were gathered. One or two made way for him in the doorway, but did not speak. Roy Blakeley was sitting on the edge of Dory's couch.

"Roy," said Tom, still hesitating in the doorway of his own patrol cabin, "can I speak to you a minute?"

Roy came out and silently followed Tom to a point out of hearing of the others.

"I—I don't care so much what the others think," said Tom. "If they want to think I'm a coward, all right. But I want to tell *you* how it was so *you* won't think so."

"Oh, you needn't mind about me," said Roy.

"You and Garry—I—"

"I guess *he* knows what to think, too," said Roy, coldly. "I guess he has his opinion of the First Bridgeboro Troop's courage."

"That's why I care most," said Tom, "on account of disgrace for one being disgrace for all—and honor, too. But there's something—"

"Well, you should have thought of that," Roy interrupted impetuously, "when you stood there and let a strange fellow rescue one of your own patrol. You practically asked him to do it—everybody saw."

"There's something—"

"Oh, sure, *there's something*! I suppose you'll be able to dig something out of the Handbook, defending cowards! You're great on the Handbook."

Again that something came up in Tom's throat and the ugly word cut him so that he could hardly speak.

"No, there isn't anything in the Manual about it," said he, in his slow monotone, "because I looked."

Roy sneered audibly.

"But I thought there might be another law—a 13th

one about—"

"Oh, you make me sick with your 13th law!" Roy flared up. "Is that what you were dreaming about when you stood on the end of that board and beckoned to Garry—"

"I didn't beckon, I just looked—"

"Just looked! Well, I don't claim to be up on the law like you, but the 10th law's good enough for me,—'A scout is brave; he has the courage to face danger in spite of fear.' This fellow will have the bronze cross, maybe the silver one, for rescuing one of *our* troop, one of *your own* patrol. *You* know how we made a resolution that the first honor medal should come to us! And here you stand there watching and let a stranger walk away with it!"

"Do you think he'll get it?" Tom asked.

"Of course, he'll get it."

Tom smiled slightly. "And *you* think I'm a coward?"

"I'm not saying what I think. I never *did* think so before. I know that fellow will have the cross and they'll be the honor troop because in *our* troop we've got—"

"Don't say that again, Roy; please don't—I—"

Roy looked at him for one moment; perhaps in that brief space all the history of their friendship came rushing back upon him, and he was on the point of stretching out his hand and letting Tom explain. But the impulse passed like a sudden storm, and he walked away.

Tom watched him until he entered the patrol shack, and then

went on to his own cabin. Jeb Rushmore was out with the class in tracking, teaching them how to *feel* a trail, and Tom sat down on his own couch, glad to be alone. He thought of the members of his own troop, in and about his own patrol cabin, ministering to Dory Bronson. He wondered what they were saying about him and whether Roy would discuss him with others. He didn't think Roy would do that. He wondered what Mr. Ellsworth would think—and Jeb Rushmore.

He got up and, fumbling in his duffel bag, fished out the thumbed and dilapidated Handbook, which was his trusty friend and companion. He opened it at page 64. He knew the place well enough, for he had many times coveted what was offered there. There, standing at attention and looking straight at him, was the picture of a scout, very trim and natty, looking, as he had often thought, exactly like Roy. Beside it was another picture of a scout tying knots and he recalled how Roy had taught him the various knots. His eyes scanned the type above till he found what he sought.

"The bronze medal is mounted on a red ribbon and is awarded to a scout who has actually saved life where risk is involved.

"The silver medal is mounted on a blue ribbon and is awarded to a scout who saves life with considerable risk to himself.

"The gold medal is mounted on white ribbon and is the highest possible award for heroism. It may be granted to a scout who has gravely endangered his own life in actually saving the life of another."

"It'll mean the silver one for him, all right," said Tom to himself, "and that's three more weeks. I wish it could be the gold one."

Idly he ran through the pages of the book, pausing here and there. On page 349 were pictures of scouts rescuing drowning persons. He knew the methods well and looked at the pictures wistfully. Again at page 278 was some matter about tracking, with notes in facsimile handwriting. This put the idea into his mind that he might insert a little handwriting of his own at a certain place, and he turned to the pages he knew best of all—33 and 34. He read the whole twelve laws, but none seemed quite to cover his case. So he wrote in a very cramped hand after Law 12 these words:

"13—A scout can make a sacrifice. He can keep from winning a medal so somebody else can get it. Especially he must do this if it does the other scout more good. That is better than being a hero."

He turned to the fly leaf and wrote in sprawling, reckless fashion: "I am not a coward. I hate cowards." Then he tore the page out and threw it away. He hardly knew what he was doing. After a few minutes he turned to page 58, where the picture of the honor medal was. As he sat gazing at it, loud shouting arose in the distance. Nearer and nearer it came, and louder it grew, until it swelled into a lusty chorus. Around the corner of the pavilion they came, two score or more of scouts, yelling and throwing their hats into the air. Tom looked up and listened. Through the little window he could glimpse them as they passed, carrying Garry Everson upon their shoulders, and shrieking themselves hoarse. Peewee was there and Artie Val Arlen, of the Ravens, and the little sandy-haired fellow with the cough, running to keep up and yelling proudly for his chief and idol.

"Hurrah for the silver cross!" they called.

"Three cheers for the honor scout!"

"Three cheers and three extra weeks!"

They paused within a dozen feet of where Tom sat, and pushing, elbowing, fell into the woods path leading up to Hero Cabin. Tom listened until their voices, spent by the distance, were scarcely audible. Then he fell to gazing again at the picture of the medal.

CHAPTER XVI

OSTRACIZED

The question was as to the bronze cross or the silver one, and it was the silver one which came. Roy, who had been the most observant witness, testified before the Honor Court that the frantic struggling of the rescued scout must have incurred danger to the rescuer and that only his dexterity and skill had saved him.

But after all, who can say how much risk is involved in such an act. It is only in those deeds of sublime recklessness where one throws his life into the balance as a tree casts off a dried leaf that the true measure of peril is known. That is where insanity and heroism seem to join hands. And hence the glittering cross of the yellow metal lying against its satin background of spotless white stands alone by itself, apart from all other awards.

There was no thought of it here and least of all by Garry himself. When asked by the court how much he believed he had jeopardized his life, he said he did not know, and that at the time he had thought only of saving Dory Bronson. He added that all scouts know the different life-saving "wrinkles" and that they have to use their judgment. His manner had a touch of nonchalance, or rather, perhaps of indifference, which struck one or two of the visiting scout-masters unfavorably. But Jeb Rushmore, who was in the room, sitting far back with his lanky arms clasped about his lanky limbs, and a shrewd look in his eyes, was greatly impressed, and it was largely because of his voice that the recommendation went to headquarters for the silver medal. In all of the proceedings the name of Tom Slade was not once mentioned, though his vantage point on the spring-board ought to have made his testimony of some value.

So Garry Everson and his little one-patrol troop took up their abode in Hero Cabin, and the little sandy-haired fellow with the cough raised and lowered the colors each day, as Tom had done, and ate more heartily down at mess, and made birchbark ornaments in the sunshine up at his beloved retreat, and was very proud of his leader; but he had little use for Tom Slade, because he believed Tom was a coward.

In due time the Silver Cross itself came, and scouts who strolled up to visit the cabin on the precipice noticed that sometimes the little sandy-haired fellow wore it, so that it came to be rumored about that Garry Everson cared more about him than he did about the medal. There were times when Garry took his meals up to him and often he was not at campfire in the evenings. But the little fellow improved each day and every one noticed it.

In time the feeling toward Tom subsided until nothing was left of it except a kind of passive disregard of him. Organized resentment would not have been tolerated at Temple Camp and it is a question whether the scouts themselves would have had anything to do with such a conspiracy. But the feeling had changed toward him and was especially noticeable in certain quarters.

Perhaps if he had lived among his own troop and patrol as

one of them the estrangement would have been entirely forgotten, but he lived a life apart, seeing them only at intervals, and so the coldness continued. As the time drew near for the troop to leave, Tom fancied that the feeling against him was stronger because they were thinking of the extra time they might have had along with the honor they had lost, but he was sensitive and possibly imagined that. He sometimes wondered if Roy and the others were gratified to know that these good friends of their happy journey to camp could remain longer. But the camp was so large and the Honor Troop stayed so much by itself that the Bridgeboro boys hardly realized what it meant to that little patrol up at Hero Cabin. Tom often thought wistfully of the pleasant cruise up the river and wondered if Roy and Pee-wee thought of it as they made their plans to go home in the *Good Turn*.

Two friends Tom had, at all events, and these were Jeb Rushmore and Garry Everson. The Honor Troop was composed mostly of small boys and all except the little boy who was Garry's especial charge were in Tom's tracking class. He used to put them through the simpler stunts and then turn them over to Jeb Rushmore. Apparently, they did not share the general prejudice and he liked to be with them.

One afternoon he returned with three or four of these youngsters and lingered on the hill to chat with Garry. He had come to feel more at home here than anywhere else.

"How's the kid?" Tom asked, as the sandy haired boy came out of the cabin and passed him without speaking.

"Fine. You ought to see him eat. He's a whole famine in himself. You mustn't mind him," he added; "he has notions."

"Oh," said Tom, "I'm used to being snubbed. It just amuses me in his case."

"How's tracking?"

"Punk. There's so much dust you can't make a track. What we need is rain, so we can get some good plain prints. That's the only way to teach a tenderfoot. Jeb says dust ought to be good enough, but he's a fiend."

"He could track an aeroplane," said Garry. "Everything's pretty dry, I guess."

"You'd say so," said Tom, "if you were down through those east woods. You could light a twig with a sun glass. They're having forest fires up back of Tannerstown."

"I saw the smoke," said Garry.

"There's a couple of hoboes down the cut a ways; we tracked them today, cooking over a loose fire. I tried to get them to cut it out; told 'em they'd have the whole woods started. They only laughed. I'm going to report it to J. R."

"They on the camp land?"

"If they were they'd have been off before this."

They strolled out to the edge of the cut and looked off across the country beyond where the waning sunlight fell upon the dense woods, touching the higher trees with its lurid glow. Over that way smoke arose and curled away in the first twilight.

"There's some good timber gone to kindling wood over there," said Garry.

"It's going to blow up to-night," said Tom; "look at the flag."

Percy K. Fitzhugh

They watched the banner as it fluttered and spread in the freshening breeze.

"Looks pretty, don't it?" said Tom. "Shall we haul it down?"

"No, let the kid do it."

Garry called and the little fellow came over for the task he loved.

"Sunset," said Garry. "Now just look at his muscle," he added, winking at Tom. "By the time this precious three weeks is up, he'll be a regular Samson."

Garry walked a few paces down the hill with Tom. "I wish I could have had a chance to thank Mr. Temple when he was here," he said, "for this bully camp and that extra time arrangement."

"He deserves thanks," said Tom.

They walked on for a few moments in silence.

"You—*you* don't think I'm a coward, do you?" said Tom, suddenly. "I wouldn't speak about it to anyone but you. But I can't help thinking about it sometimes. I wouldn't speak about it even to Roy—now."

"Of course, I don't. I think you were a little rattled, that's all. I've been the same myself. For a couple of seconds you didn't know what to do—you were just up in the air—and by the time you got a grip on yourself—I had cheated you out of it. You were just going to dive, weren't you?"

"Sometimes it's hard to make a fellow understand," said Tom, not answering the question. "I can't tell you just what I was thinking. That's my own business. I—I've got it in my Handbook. But all I want to know is, *you* don't think I'm a coward, do you?"

"Sure, I don't."

Garry turned back and Tom went on down the winding path through the woods to camp. The breeze, becoming brisker, blew the leaves this way and that, and as he plodded on through the dusk he had to lower his head to keep his hat from blowing off. The wind brought with it a faint but pungent odor which reminded him of the autumn days at home when he and Roy raked up the leaves and burned them behind the Blakeley house. He avoided this train of thought. His face was stolid, and his manner dogged as he hurried on, with the rather clumsy gait which still bore the faintest trace of the old shuffle Barrel Alley had known so well.

Near the camp he ran plunk into Roy.

"Hello," he said.

"Hello," said Roy, and passed on.

"Roy," Tom called after him, "I want to speak to you a minute."

Roy paused.

"I—I was thinking—do you smell smoke, Roy? It makes me think how we used to rake up the leaves."

Roy said nothing.

"I understand the troop is going home tomorrow and some of you are going in the *Good Turn*. I hope you'll have a fine trip

—like when we came up. I wish you could all stay longer. It makes me kind of homesick to see you all go."

"We might have stayed longer," said Roy, coldly, "only—is that all you want to say to me?" he broke off.

"I just want to say good-bye and—"

"All right, good-bye," said Roy, and walked away.

Tom watched him for a few seconds, then went on down to supper.

CHAPTER XVII

THE WINNING OF THE GOLDEN CROSS

The wind had become so strong that it was necessary to move the mess boards around to the leeward side of the pavilion. Several fellows remarked on the pungent odor which permeated the air and a couple who had been stalking spoke of the woods fires over beyond Tannerstown.

Garry was not at supper, nor the little sandy-haired fellow, but the others of his patrol came down before the meal was over.

"Guess we'll cut out yarns to-night," said Jeb Rushmore, "and hike out on a little tour of inspection."

"There are a couple of tramps in the woods this side of the cut, right up the hill a ways," said Tom.

"We need rain, that's sure," said another scout.

"Maybe we'll get some with this wind," remarked another.

"No, I reckon it's a dry wind," said Mr. Rushmore, looking about and sniffing audibly. "Gol smash it," he added, rising and sniffing still louder. "Thar's somethin' in the air."

Percy K. Fitzhugh

For a minute he stood near his place, then strode off up the hill a little way, among the trees, where he paused, listening, like an animal at bay. They could see his dark form dimly outlined in the darker night.

"J. R.'s on the scent," remarked Doc. Carson.

Several fellows rose to join him and just at that minute Westy Martin, of the Silver Foxes, and a scout from a Maryland troop who had been stalking, came rushing pell-mell into camp.

"The woods are on fire!" gasped Westy. "Up the hill! Look!"

"I seed it," said Jeb. "The wind's bringin' it."

"You can't get through up there," Westy panted. "We had to go around."

"Ye couldn't get round by now. B'ys, we're a-goin' ter git it for sure. It's goin' ter blow fire."

For a moment he stood looking up into the woods, with the boys about him, straining their eyes to see the patches of fire which were visible here and there. Suddenly these patches seemed to merge and make the night lurid with a red glare, a perfect pandemonium of crackling and roaring assailed the silent night and clouds of suffocating smoke enveloped them.

The fire, like some heartless savage beast, had stolen upon them unawares and was ready to spring.

Jeb Rushmore was calm and self-contained and so were most of the boys as they stood ready to do his bidding.

"Naow, ye see what I meant when I said a leopard's as

sneaky as a fire," said Jeb. "Here, you Bridgeboro troop and them two Maryland troops and the troop from Washin't'n," he called, "you make a bucket line like we practiced. Tom— whar's Tom? And you Oakwood b'ys, git the buckets out'n the provish'n camp. Line up thar ri' down t' the water's edge and come up through here. You fellers from Pennsylvany 'n' you others thar, git the axes 'n' come 'long o' me. Don't git rattled, now."

Like clockwork they formed a line from the lake up around the camp, completely encircling it. The fire crept nearer every second, stifling them with its pungent smoke. Other scouts, some with long axes, others with belt axes, followed Jeb Rushmore, chopping down the small trees which he indicated along the path made by this human line. In less than a minute fifty or more scouts were working desperately felling trees along the path. Fortunately, the trees were small, and fortunately, too, the scouts knew how to fell them so that they fell in each case away from the path, leaving an open way behind the camp.

Along this open way the line stood, and thus the full buckets passing from hand to hand with almost the precision of machinery, were emptied along this open area, soaking it.

"The rest o' you b'ys," called Jeb, "climb up on the cabins— one on each cabin, and three or four uv ye on the pavilion. Some o' ye stay below to pass the buckets up. Keep the roofs wet—that's whar the sparks'll light. Hey, Tom!"

As the hurried work went on one of Garry's troop grasped Jeb by the arm. "How about our cabin?" said he, fearfully. "There are two fellows up there."

Jeb paused a moment, but shook his head. "They'll hev ter risk jumpin' int' th' cut," said he. "No mortal man c'u'd git to 'em through them woods naow."

The boy fell back, sick at heart as he thought of those two on the lonely hill surrounded by flame and with a leap from the precipice as their only alternative. It was simply a choice between two forms of awful death.

The fire had now swept to within a few yards of the outer edge of the camp, but an open way had been cleared and saturated to check its advance and the roofs of the shacks were kept soaked by a score or more of alert workers as a precaution against the blowing sparks.

Tom Slade had not answered any of Jeb's calls for him. At the time of his chief's last summons he was a couple of hundred feet from the buildings, tearing and tugging at one of the overflow tents. Like a madman and with a strength born of desperation he dragged the pole down and, wrenching the stakes out of the ground by main force, never stopping to untie the ropes, he hauled the whole dishevelled mass free of the paraphernalia which had been beneath it, down to the lake. Duffel bags rolled out from under it, the uprooted stakes which came along with it caught among trees and were torn away, the long clumsy canvas trail rebelled and clung to many an obstruction, only to be torn and ripped as it was hauled willy-nilly to the shore of the lake.

In he strode, tugging, wrenching, dragging it after him. Part of it floated because of the air imprisoned beneath it, but gradually sank as it became soaked. Standing knee-deep, he held fast to one corner of it and waited during one precious minute while it absorbed as much of the water as it could hold.

It was twice as heavy now, but he was twice as strong, for he was twice as desperate and had the strength of an uncon-querable purpose. The lips of his big mouth were drawn tight, his shock of hair hung about his stolid face as with bulldog strength and tenacity he dragged the dead weight of dripping canvas after him up onto the shore. The water trickled out of its clinging folds as he raised one side of the soaking fabric, and dragged the whole mass up to the provision cabin.

He seized the coil of lasso rope and hung it around his neck, then raising the canvas, he pulled it over his head like a shawl and pinned it about him with the steel clutch of his fingers, one hand at neck and one below.

Up through the blazing woods he started with the leaden weight of this dripping winding sheet upon him and catching in the hubbly obstructions in his path. The water streamed down his face and he felt the chill of it as it permeated his clothes, but that was well—it was his only friend and ally now.

Like some ghostly bride he stumbled up through the lurid night, dragging the unwieldly train behind him. Apparently no one saw this strange apparition as it disappeared amid the enveloping flames.

"Tom—whar's Tom?" called Jeb Rushmore again.

Up the hill he went, tearing his dripping armor when it caught, and pausing at last to lift the soaking train and wind that about him also.

The crackling flames gathering about him like a pack of hungry wolves hissed as they lapped against his wet shroud, and drew back, baffled, only to assail him again. The trail was narrow and the flames close on either side.

Once, twice, the drying fabric was aflame, but he wrapped it under wetter folds. His face was burning hot; he strove with might and main against the dreadful faintness caused by the heat, and the smoke all but suffocated him.

On and up he pressed, stooping and sometimes almost creeping, for it was easier near the ground. Now he held the drying canvas with his teeth and beat with his hands to extinguish the persistent flames. His power of resistance was all but gone and as he realized it his heart sank within him. At last, stooping like some sneaking thing, he reached the sparser growth near the cut.

Two boys who had been driven to the verge of the precipice and lingered there in dread of the alternative they must take, saw a strange sight. A dull gray mass, with two ghostly hands reaching out and slapping at it, and a wild-eyed face completely framed by its charred and blackening shroud, emerged from amid the fire and smoke and came straight toward them.

"What is it?" whispered the younger boy, drawing closer to Garry in momentary fright at the sight of this spectral thing.

"Don't jump—it's me—Tom Slade! Here, take this rope, quick. I guess it isn't burned any. I meant to wet it, too," he gasped. "Is that tree solid? I can't seem to see. All right, quick! I can't do it. Make a loop and put it under his arms and let him down."

There was not a minute to spare, and no time for explanations or questions. Garry lowered the boy into the cut.

"Now you'll have to let me down, I'm afraid," said Tom. "My hands are funny and I can't—I can't go hand over hand."

"That's easy," said Garry.

But it was not so easy as it had been to lower the smaller boy. He had to encircle the tree twice with the rope to guard against a too rapid descent, and to smooth the precipice where the rope went over the edge to keep it from cutting. When Tom had been lowered into the cut, Garry himself went down hand over hand.

It was cool down there, but they could hear the wild flames raging above and many sparks descended and died on the already burned surface. The air blew in a strong, refreshing draught through the deep gully, and the three boys, hardly realizing their hair-breadth escape, seemed to be in a different world, or rather, in the cellar of the world above, which was being swept by that heartless roistering wind and fire.

* * * * *

Along through the cut they came, a dozen or more scarred and weary scouts, their clothing in tatters, anxious and breathing heavily. They had come by the long way around the edge of the woods and got into the cut where the hill was low and the gully shallow.

"Is anyone there?" a scout called, as they neared the point above which Hero Cabin had stood. They knew well enough that no one could be left alive above.

"We're here," called Garry.

"Hurt? Did you jump—both of you?"

"Three, the kid and I and Tom Slade."

"Tom Slade? How did *he* get here?"

"Came up through the woods and brought us a rope. *We're* all right, but he's played out. Got a stretcher?"

"Sure."

They came up, swinging their lanterns, to where Tom lay on the ground with Garry's jacket folded under his head for a pillow, and they listened soberly to Garry's simple tale of the strange, shrouded apparition that had emerged from the flames with the precious life line coiled about its neck.

It was hard to believe, but there were the cold facts, and they could only stand about, silent and aghast at what they heard.

"We missed him," said one scout.

"Is the camp saved?" asked Garry.

"Mostly, but we had a stiff job."

"Don't talk about *our* job," said Doc Carson as he stooped, holding the lantern before Tom's blackened face and taking his wrist to feel the pulse.

Again there was silence as they all stood about and the little sandy-haired fellow with the cough crept close to the prostrate form and gazed, fascinated, into that stolid, homely face.

And still no one spoke.

"It means the gold cross," someone whispered.

"Do you think the gold cross is good enough?" Garry asked, quietly.

"It's the best we have."

Then Roy, who was among them, kneeled down and put his arm out toward Tom.

"Don't touch my hand," said Tom, faintly. "It isn't that I don't want to shake hands with you," he added. "I wanted to do that when I met you—before supper. Only my hands feel funny—tingly, kind of—and they hurt.

"Any of my own patrol here?" he asked after a moment.

"Yes, Connie Bennett's here—and Will Bronson."

"Then I'd rather have them carry the stretcher, and I'd like for you to walk along by me—I got something to say to you."

They did as he asked, the others following at a little distance, except the little sandy-haired boy who persisted in running forward until Garry called him back and kept his own deterring arm about the boy's shoulder.

"I don't mind my own patrol hearing—or you. I don't care about the gold cross. It's only what it means that counts—sort of. I let Garry save your brother, Will, because I knew he needed to stay longer—I knew about that kid not being strong—that's all. I can go through water as easy as I can through fire—it's—it's easier—if it comes to that."

"Don't try to talk, Tom," said Roy, brokenly.

"But I wouldn't tell even you, Roy, because—because if he'd found it out he wouldn't think it was fair—and he wouldn't have taken it. That's the kind of a fellow he is, Roy."

"Yes, I know what kind of a fellow he is," said Roy.

"Anyway, it's no matter now. You see yourself Hero Cabin is burned down. A fellow might—he might even lose the cross. It's the three weeks that counted—see?"

"Yes, I see," said Roy.

"And tomorrow I want to go back with you fellows in the *Good Turn*—and see Mr. Temple. I want to ask him if that kid can stay with Jeb 'till Christmas. Then I'll come back up to camp. I've thought a lot lately about our trip up in the *Good Turn*, Roy."

"Yes—so have I, Tom. But don't talk now. Doc doesn't want you to."

"We've got to find Harry Stanton," said Tom, after a few minutes.

"Yes," said Roy.

But whether they ever did find him and the singular adventures attending their quest, are really part of another story.

THE END

Other books by this author

Tom Slade at Black Lake

Tom Slade's Double Dare

Tom Slade with the Boys Over There

Tom Slade with the Colors

Tom Slade Motorcycle Dispatch Bearer

Tom Slade Mystery Trail

Pee-Wee Harris on the Trail

Pee-Wee Harris Adrift

Roy Blakeley's Adventures in Camp

Roy Blakeley

Percy K. Fitzhugh

Choose from Thousands of 1stWorldLibrary Classics By

A. M. Barnard
Ada Leverson
Adolphus William Ward
Aesop
Agatha Christie
Alexander Aaronsohn
Alexander Kielland
Alexandre Dumas
Alfred Gatty
Alfred Ollivant
Alice Duer Miller
Alice Turner Curtis
Alice Dunbar
Allen Chapman
Alleyne Ireland
Ambrose Bierce
Amelia E. Barr
Amory H. Bradford
Andrew Lang
Andrew McFarland Davis
Andy Adams
Angela Brazil
Anna Alice Chapin
Anna Sewell
Annie Besant
Annie Hamilton Donnell
Annie Payson Call
Annie Roe Carr
Annonaymous
Anton Chekhov
Archibald Lee Fletcher
Arnold Bennett
Arthur C. Benson
Arthur Conan Doyle
Arthur M. Winfield
Arthur Ransome
Arthur Schnitzler
Arthur Train
Atticus
B.H. Baden-Powell
B. M. Bower
B. C. Chatterjee
Baroness Emmuska Orczy
Baroness Orczy
Basil King
Bayard Taylor
Ben Macomber
Bertha Muzzy Bower
Bjornstjerne Bjornson

Booth Tarkington
Boyd Cable
Bram Stoker
C. Collodi
C. E. Orr
C. M. Ingleby
Carolyn Wells
Catherine Parr Traill
Charles A. Eastman
Charles Amory Beach
Charles Dickens
Charles Dudley Warner
Charles Farrar Browne
Charles Ives
Charles Kingsley
Charles Klein
Charles Hanson Towne
Charles Lathrop Pack
Charles Romyn Dake
Charles Whibley
Charles Willing Beale
Charlotte M. Braeme
Charlotte M. Yonge
Charlotte Perkins Stetson
Clair W. Hayes
Clarence Day Jr.
Clarence E. Mulford
Clemence Housman
Confucius
Coningsby Dawson
Cornelis DeWitt Wilcox
Cyril Burleigh
D. H. Lawrence
Daniel Defoe
David Garnett
Dinah Craik
Don Carlos Janes
Donald Keyhoe
Dorothy Kilner
Dougan Clark
Douglas Fairbanks
E. Nesbit
E. P. Roe
E. Phillips Oppenheim
E. S. Brooks
Earl Barnes
Edgar Rice Burroughs
Edith Van Dyne
Edith Wharton

Edward Everett Hale
Edward J. O'Biren
Edward S. Ellis
Edwin L. Arnold
Eleanor Atkins
Eleanor Hallowell Abbott
Eliot Gregory
Elizabeth Gaskell
Elizabeth McCracken
Elizabeth Von Arnim
Ellem Key
Emerson Hough
Emilie F. Carlen
Emily Bronte
Emily Dickinson
Enid Bagnold
Enilor Macartney Lane
Erasmus W. Jones
Ernie Howard Pie
Ethel May Dell
Ethel Turner
Ethel Watts Mumford
Eugene Sue
Eugenie Foa
Eugene Wood
Eustace Hale Ball
Evelyn Everett-green
Everard Cotes
F. H. Cheley
F. J. Cross
F. Marion Crawford
Fannie E. Newberry
Federick Austin Ogg
Ferdinand Ossendowski
Fergus Hume
Florence A. Kilpatrick
Fremont B. Deering
Francis Bacon
Francis Darwin
Frances Hodgson Burnett
Frances Parkinson Keyes
Frank Gee Patchin
Frank Harris
Frank Jewett Mather
Frank L. Packard
Frank V. Webster
Frederic Stewart Isham
Frederick Trevor Hill
Frederick Winslow Taylor

Friedrich Kerst	Hayden Carruth	James Branch Cabell
Friedrich Nietzsche	Helent Hunt Jackson	James DeMille
Fyodor Dostoyevsky	Helen Nicolay	James Joyce
G.A. Henty	Hendrik Conscience	James Lane Allen
G.K. Chesterton	Hendy David Thoreau	James Lane Allen
Gabrielle E. Jackson	Henri Barbusse	James Oliver Curwood
Garrett P. Serviss	Henrik Ibsen	James Oppenheim
Gaston Leroux	Henry Adams	James Otis
George A. Warren	Henry Ford	James R. Driscoll
George Ade	Henry Frost	Jane Abbott
Geroge Bernard Shaw	Henry James	Jane Austen
George Cary Eggleston	Henry Jones Ford	Jane L. Stewart
George Durston	Henry Seton Merriman	Janet Aldridge
George Ebers	Henry W Longfellow	Jens Peter Jacobsen
George Eliot	Herbert A. Giles	Jerome K. Jerome
George Gissing	Herbert Carter	Jessie Graham Flower
George MacDonald	Herbert N. Casson	John Buchan
George Meredith	Herman Hesse	John Burroughs
George Orwell	Hildegard G. Frey	John Cournos
George Sylvester Viereck	Homer	John F. Kennedy
George Tucker	Honore De Balzac	John Gay
George W. Cable	Horace B. Day	John Glasworthy
George Wharton James	Horace Walpole	John Habberton
Gertrude Atherton	Horatio Alger Jr.	John Joy Bell
Gordon Casserly	Howard Pyle	John Kendrick Bangs
Grace E. King	Howard R. Garis	John Milton
Grace Gallatin	Hugh Lofting	John Philip Sousa
Grace Greenwood	Hugh Walpole	John Taintor Foote
Grant Allen	Humphry Ward	Jonas Lauritz Idemil Lie
Guillermo A. Sherwell	Ian Maclaren	Jonathan Swift
Gulielma Zollinger	Inez Haynes Gillmore	Joseph A. Altsheler
Gustav Flaubert	Irving Bacheller	Joseph Carey
H. A. Cody	Isabel Cecilia Williams	Joseph Conrad
H. B. Irving	Isabel Hornibrook	Joseph E. Badger Jr
H. C. Bailey	Israel Abrahams	Joseph Hergesheimer
H. G. Wells	Ivan Turgenev	Joseph Jacobs
H. H. Munro	J. G.Austin	Jules Vernes
H. Irving Hancock	J. Henri Fabre	Julian Hawthrone
H. R. Naylor	J. M. Barrie	Julie A Lippmann
H. Rider Haggard	J. M. Walsh	Justin Huntly McCarthy
H. W. C. Davis	J. Macdonald Oxley	Kakuzo Okakura
Haldeman Julius	J. R. Miller	Karle Wilson Baker
Hall Caine	J. S. Fletcher	Kate Chopin
Hamilton Wright Mabie	J. S. Knowles	Kenneth Grahame
Hans Christian Andersen	J. Storer Clouston	Kenneth McGaffey
Harold Avery	J. W. Duffield	Kate Langley Bosher
Harold McGrath	Jack London	Kate Langley Bosher
Harriet Beecher Stowe	Jacob Abbott	Katherine Cecil Thurston
Harry Castlemon	James Allen	Katherine Stokes
Harry Coghill	James Andrews	L. A. Abbot
Harry Houidini	James Baldwin	L. T. Meade

L. Frank Baum	Paul G. Tomlinson	T. S. Arthur
Latta Griswold	Paul Severing	The Princess Der Ling
Laura Dent Crane	Percy Brebner	Thomas A. Janvier
Laura Lee Hope	Percy Keese Fitzhugh	Thomas A Kempis
Laurence Housman	Peter B. Kyne	Thomas Anderton
Lawrence Beasley	Plato	Thomas Bailey Aldrich
Leo Tolstoy	Quincy Allen	Thomas Bulfinch
Leonid Andreyev	R. Derby Holmes	Thomas De Quincey
Lewis Carroll	R. L. Stevenson	Thomas Dixon
Lewis Sperry Chafer	R. S. Ball	Thomas H. Huxley
Lilian Bell	Rabindranath Tagore	Thomas Hardy
Lloyd Osbourne	Rahul Alvares	Thomas More
Louis Hughes	Ralph Bonehill	Thornton W. Burgess
Louis Joseph Vance	Ralph Henry Barbour	U. S. Grant
Louis Tracy	Ralph Victor	Upton Sinclair
Louisa May Alcott	Ralph Waldo Emmerson	Valentine Williams
Lucy Fitch Perkins	Rene Descartes	Various Authors
Lucy Maud Montgomery	Ray Cummings	Vaughan Kester
Luther Benson	Rex Beach	Victor Appleton
Lydia Miller Middleton	Rex E. Beach	Victor G. Durham
Lyndon Orr	Richard Harding Davis	Victoria Cross
M. Corvus	Richard Jefferies	Virginia Woolf
M. H. Adams	Richard Le Gallienne	Wadsworth Camp
Margaret E. Sangster	Robert Barr	Walter Camp
Margret Howth	Robert Frost	Walter Scott
Margaret Vandercook	Robert Gordon Anderson	Washington Irving
Margaret W. Hungerford	Robert L. Drake	Wilbur Lawton
Margret Penrose	Robert Lansing	Wilkie Collins
Maria Edgeworth	Robert Lynd	Willa Cather
Maria Thompson Daviess	Robert Michael Ballantyne	Willard F. Baker
Mariano Azuela	Robert W. Chambers	William Dean Howells
Marion Polk Angellotti	Rosa Nouchette Carey	William le Queux
Mark Overton	Rudyard Kipling	W. Makepeace Thackeray
Mark Twain	Saint Augustine	William W. Walter
Mary Austin	Samuel B. Allison	William Shakespeare
Mary Catherine Crowley	Samuel Hopkins Adams	Winston Churchill
Mary Cole	Sarah Bernhardt	Yei Theodora Ozaki
Mary Hastings Bradley	Sarah C. Hallowell	Yogi Ramacharaka
Mary Roberts Rinehart	Selma Lagerlof	Young E. Allison
Mary Rowlandson	Sherwood Anderson	Zane Grey
M. Wollstonecraft Shelley	Sigmund Freud	
Maud Lindsay	Standish O'Grady	
Max Beerbohm	Stanley Weyman	
Myra Kelly	Stella Benson	
Nathaniel Hawthrone	Stella M. Francis	
Nicolo Machiavelli	Stephen Crane	
O. F. Walton	Stewart Edward White	
Oscar Wilde	Stijn Streuvels	
Owen Johnson	Swami Abhedananda	
P.G. Wodehouse	Swami Parmananda	
Paul and Mabel Thorne	T. S. Ackland	

www.ingramcontent.com/pod-product-compliance
Lightning Source LLC
Chambersburg PA
CBHW051823170626
46807CB00003B/1004